EXAM TRAINING
Business Milestones
Englisch für kaufmännische Berufe

Workbook für alle kaufmännischen Ausgaben mit
Prüfungsvorbereitung KMK-Fremdsprachenzertifikat

Ruth Feiertag
Dr. Richard Hooton
Ulrike Krabbe
Uwe Krabbe

Ernst Klett Verlag
Stuttgart · Leipzig

Übungen zu Units 1–16

Prüfungsvorbereitung KMK-Fremdsprachenzertifikat

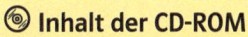

◉ Inhalt der CD-ROM

Audio-Tracks
Lösungsvorschläge zu den Aufgaben im Workbook

Zeichenerklärung

◉ A 3.1   CD-ROM, Track 3.1

!   Hinweis auf typische Fehler
und Tipps

Übungen zu Units 1–16

Der erste Teil des Workbooks bietet Ihnen die Möglichkeit, die im Schülerbuch vermittelten Kenntnisse und Fertigkeiten zu vertiefen. Die einzelnen Units des Workbooks lehnen sich eng an die jeweilige Unit des Schülerbuchs an und die Aufgaben nehmen darauf Bezug.

Die Units des Workbooks sind in drei Abschnitte gegliedert:

1. Unit refresher

Dieser Teil enthält vertiefende Übungen zum Thema der Unit. Hier können Sie den im Schülerbuch vermittelten Lernstoff durch Hörverstehensaufgaben zu authentischen Dialogen sowie durch die Produktion von Korrespondenz und das Bearbeiten von Formularen wiederholen und festigen.

2. Grammar refresher

Der Grammatikteil nimmt häufig die Grammatikdarstellung des Schülerbuches auf und führt diese weiter. Es wurde ein kontrastiver Ansatz mit begleitenden Übungen gewählt, unter besonderer Berücksichtigung der Strukturen, die speziell deutschen Lernern Schwierigkeiten bereiten. Ausrufezeichen am Rand weisen auf Kernprobleme und Tipps hin.

3. Phrases refresher

Weil Sie für gelungene Geschäftskommunikation einen sicheren Fundus von Redemitteln benötigen, schließen sich Übungen zu den *Phrases* der jeweiligen Unit des Schülerbuchs an. Hier können Sie insbesondere grammatische und idiomatische Strukturen sowie Präpositionen üben, die erfahrungs- gemäß besonderer Festigung bedürfen.

Prüfungsvorbereitung KMK-Fremdsprachenzertifikat

Die KMK-Zertifikatsprüfung hat sich mittlerweile in vielen Schulen in Deutschland etabliert. Mit ihr können Sie sich Ihre berufsbezogenen Fremdsprachenkenntnisse in einer europaweit anerkannten Form bescheinigen lassen. Auch Arbeitgeber legen verstärkt Wert auf das Ablegen dieser Prüfung, da durch die internationale Verflechtung Fremdsprachen zunehmend zum Medium der Verständigung werden und für die Berufsausübung unabdingbar sind.

Die KMK-Zertifikatsprüfung wird von den Schulen freiwillig angeboten, d. h. unabhängig von der jeweiligen Beschulung und Benotung. Sie müssen sich also vielerorts weitgehend selbstständig auf die Prüfung vorbereiten. Mit dem zweiten Teil des Workbooks möchten wir Ihnen dabei helfen.

Die *Warm up*-Übungen sollen Ihnen zeigen, wo Ihre Stärken und Schwächen liegen. Der umfassende Aufgabenteil dient dann zur gezielten Einübung der verschiedenen Aufgabentypen. Mithilfe der beigefügten CD-ROM kann auch der Aufgabentyp Rezeption – Hörverstehen geübt werden.

Alle Aufgaben innerhalb eines Aufgabentyps reichen von anfänglich einfacheren Übungen bis hin zu anspruchsvollen Aufgaben. Ebenso wurden zu den verschiedenen Aufgabentypen Bearbeitungs- hinweise formuliert, die Ihnen bei der Vorbereitung nützliche Hilfestellungen geben.

An die Übungen schließen sich vier vollständige Musterprüfungen an für die Niveaustufen I, II und III.

Zu allen Aufgaben im Workbook finden Sie Lösungsvorschläge auf der beigefügten CD-ROM. Zudem befinden sich auf der CD-ROM sämtliche Audios zum Workbook und zu den Lehrwerken.

Wir hoffen, dass Ihnen durch die vorliegende Aufgabensammlung eine umfassende Vorbereitung gelingt und wünschen Ihnen viel Erfolg in Ihrem Beruf und beim Bestehen der Prüfung.

Unit 1 Introducing yourself

Unit refresher

1 Using your imagination complete what the partners might say in the dialogues.

Partner A	Partner B
1. Hello. I'm Steven.	Hi, _____.
2. Hi, Jane. How's things?	Hello, _____?
3. My name is Nando Ngombo. _____ _____.	How do you do, Mr Ngombo? Pleased to meet you, too.
4. Good morning. My name's Robert Croft. I'm the sales manager.	Good morning. Nice _____ _____.
5. My surname is Sanchez and my first name is Diego.	My first name _____ _____.
6. I was born in Berlin but my parents come from Turkey.	I was born _____ _____.
7. I'm into _____.	My hobby is deep sea diving.
8. I love kite surfing.	I'm keen on _____.
9. I work for a wholesaler in cosmetics.	I'm training to become _____ _____.
10. I'm doing a _____ _____.	I'm training as an insurance clerk.

2
A 3.1
Sara and Adam are taking part in a careers workshop organised by the chamber of commerce and the job centre. They meet in the coffee break. Listen to their conversation and answer the following questions.

1. What does Adam think of the workshop?

    _____

    _____

2. What does Sara do job-wise?

    _____

    _____

3. When is Adam due to finish his apprenticeship?

    _____

4. Why is Sara's French so fluent?

    _____

5. What sort of course is Sara thinking of taking?

    _____

6. What is her ambition eventually?

    _____

7. Why does Adam think this course might be good for him, too?

    _____

8. Where does Sara suggest they meet?

    _____

3 Put in the words. The solutions are given in scrambled form in brackets after the blanks.

1. I'm a _____ [bakn] clerk.

2. He's training as a car sales _____ [ametgeannm] assistant.

3. She's a _____ [inatree] wholesale and _____ [oxetrp]

    clerk.

4. I'm training to _____ [becmoe] an office administration _____ [lerkc].

5. She's an _____ [uanrecnis] clerk.

6. I hope to become an IT _____ [ntncusoalt].

7. They're planning to become retail management _____ [tsiasnstas].

8. He's doing a traineeship as an _____ [lisduaitrn] clerk.

Grammar refresher

Language and grammar: Negative forms

Enthält die Verbform ein Hilfsverb (*am, is, are, was, were, have, has, had, will, would, can, must, should*) wird einfach *not* nach dem (ersten) Hilfsverb eingefügt, ähnlich wie im Deutschen.

bejaht	verneint
I am doing a traineeship.	I am not doing a traineeship.
They were informed of the change.	They were not informed of the change.
She has been waiting for them.	She has not been waiting for them.
I would like to be a bank clerk.	I would not like to be a bank clerk.

Tipp: Enthält die Verbform kein Hilfsverb, muss mithilfe von *to do* und *not* verneint werden. Person und Zeit werden mit *to do* ausgedrückt, das Hauptverb steht im Infinitiv. **!**

bejaht	verneint
They attend vocational college.	They do not attend vocational college.
He takes part in this programme.	He does not take part in this programme.
She left school last year.	She did not leave school last year.

Das Hilfsverb *must* wird mittels *to do, have to* und *not* verneint.

He must apply in writing.	He does not have to apply in writing.

1 **Make the following statements negative.**

1. I am training to become an office administration clerk.

   _____ to become an office administration clerk.

2. I like my job because I can work on my own.

   _____ my job because _____ on my own.

3. She works in the energy sector.

   _____ in the energy sector.

4. In her former job she used her English a great deal.

   In her former job _____ her English a great deal.

5. He gets on well with the people he works with.

   _____ with the people he works with.

6. They liked working with a computer.

   _____ with a computer.

7. You will be working from 9 am to 5 pm.

   You _____ from 9 am to 5 pm.

8. She is applying to train as an office management assistant.

   She _____ to train as an office management assistant.

Language and grammar: Questions

Enthält die Verbform ein Hilfsverb *(am, is, are, was, were, have, has, had, will, would, can, must, should)*, wird die Frage durch Umstellung von Satzgegenstand und Hilfsverb gebildet, ähnlich wie im Deutschen.

Aussage	Frage
He is doing a traineeship.	Is he doing a traineeship?
They were allowed to go home.	Were they allowed to go home?
I must leave early.	Must you leave early?

Tipp: Enthält die Verbform kein Hilfsverb, muss die Frage mithilfe von *to do* gebildet werden. Person und Zeit werden mit *to do* ausgedrückt, das Hauptverb steht im Infinitiv.

Aussage	Frage
They attend vocational college.	Do they attend vocational college?
He qualifies for this job.	Does he qualify for this job?
She worked hard on that project.	Did she work hard on that project?

Bildet ein Fragepronomen *(who, whose, which, what)* das Subjekt des Fragesatzes, entfällt die Umschreibung mit *to do*.

Who tried to reach us last night?	Which do you prefer, tea or coffee?
Whose car failed the test?	What products appeal to trainees?

2 **Turn the statements into questions.**

1. He is a trainee wholesale and export clerk.

   _____ a trainee wholesale and export clerk?

2. She works in the household goods industry.

   _____ in the household goods industry?

3. I took part in a re-training programme for IT consultants.

   _____ (you) in a re-training programme for IT consultants?

4. I have been working hard for this exam.

   _____ (you) hard for this exam?

5. Normally, I go to the gym before work.

   _____ (you) normally go to the gym before work?

6. He enjoyed riding along the beach.

   _____ along the beach?

7. He will be working from 9 am to 5 pm.

   _____ from 9 am to 5 pm?

8. The company has offered us a discount of 10 % on this bulk order.

   _____ a discount of 10 % on this bulk order?

bulk order – Großauftrag

3 Translate the questions into English.

1. Machst du eine Ausbildung als Industriekaufmann?

   _____

2. Wer möchte gerne Kauffrau für Bürokommunikation werden?

   _____

3. Interessieren Sie sich nicht für Computerspiele?

   _____

4. Hast du dich schon um eine Stelle beworben?

   _____

5. Müssen Sie an diesem Ausbildungsprogramm teilnehmen?

   _____

6. Wofür interessierst du dich besonders?

   _____

Phrases refresher

1 Put in the correct prepositions from the box.

> about (2x) • at • from • in (3x) • into • of • on (2x) • to

1. I work _____ Donwell Engineering plc.
2. I was born _____ Leeds _____ 17 January 1990.
3. In my new job I have to work _____ my own.
4. May I introduce Mr Summers _____ you?
5. What do you like _____ your new company?
6. She is taking part _____ a re-training programme.
7. I'm _____ deep sea diving.
8. I've heard a lot _____ you _____ Mrs Bates.
9. What industry are you _____?
10. There are no prospects _____ promotion.

2 Cross out the incorrect alternative.

1. **What/Which** are you doing job-wise?
2. I **visit/attend** vocational school two days a week.
3. **Have you met/Did you meet** Mr Cole yesterday?
4. I am training as **an insurance clerk/insurance clerk**.
5. I am in the catering **branch/industry**.
6. He works as **programmer/a programmer**.
7. I do **much/a lot of** swimming.
8. I **am/was** born on 23 March 1984.

Unit refresher

1 Fill in the crossword below. You will find the words you need in your student's book.

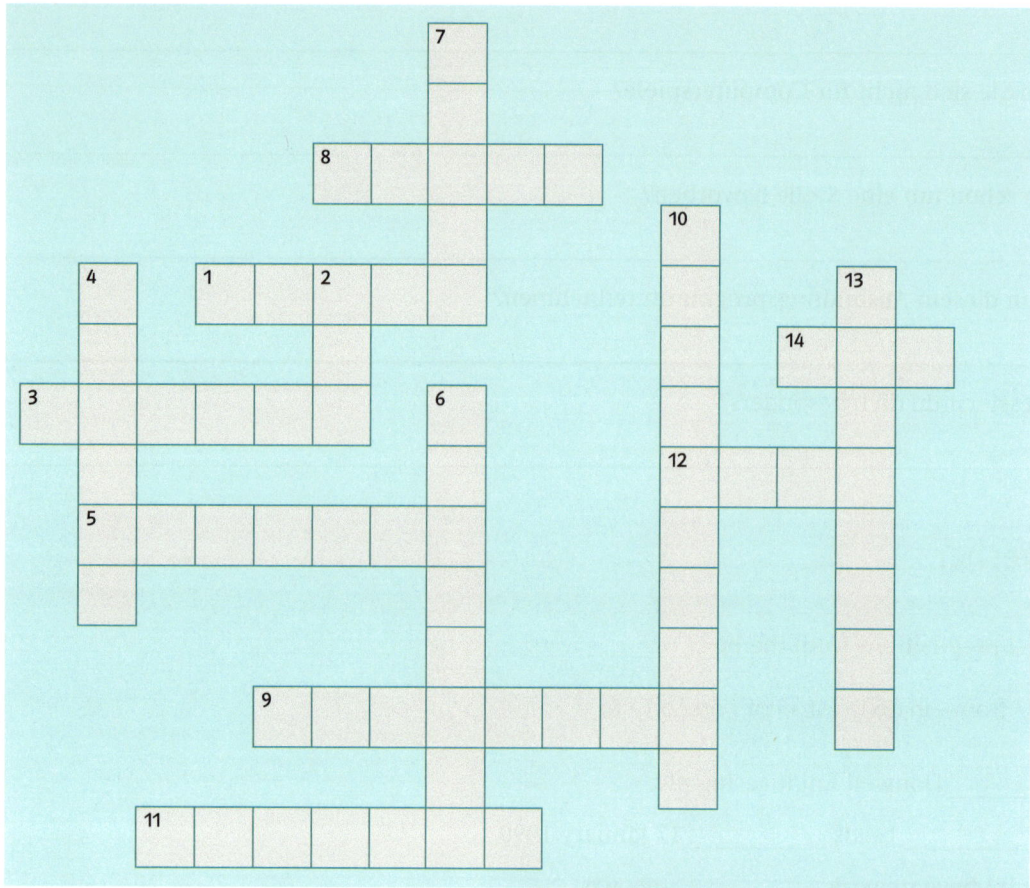

Across

1. regnerisch, verregnet
3. schön
5. Nieselregen
8. windig
9. entsetzlich
11. Klima
12. Orkan
14. Nebel

Down

2. eisig, vereist
4. Wolken
6. bedeckt
7. sonnig
10. veränderlich
13. Vorhersage

2 Tick (✓) the sentences which are safe as topics for conversation with business partners.

3
☐ How was your flight?

1
☐ The weather has been rather unsettled lately.

2
☐ What do you think of the US policies in the Middle East?

4
☐ The hotel is very quiet and the food quite good.

5
☐ Are you married?

6
☐ I'm an accountant. What's your profession?

7
☐ There are far too many immigrants living off social security in this country.

8
☐ In winter we hardly have any snow but we do have a lot of rain.

10
☐ I usually go jogging before I start work.

9
☐ I do hope this incompetent govern-ment isn't re-elected.

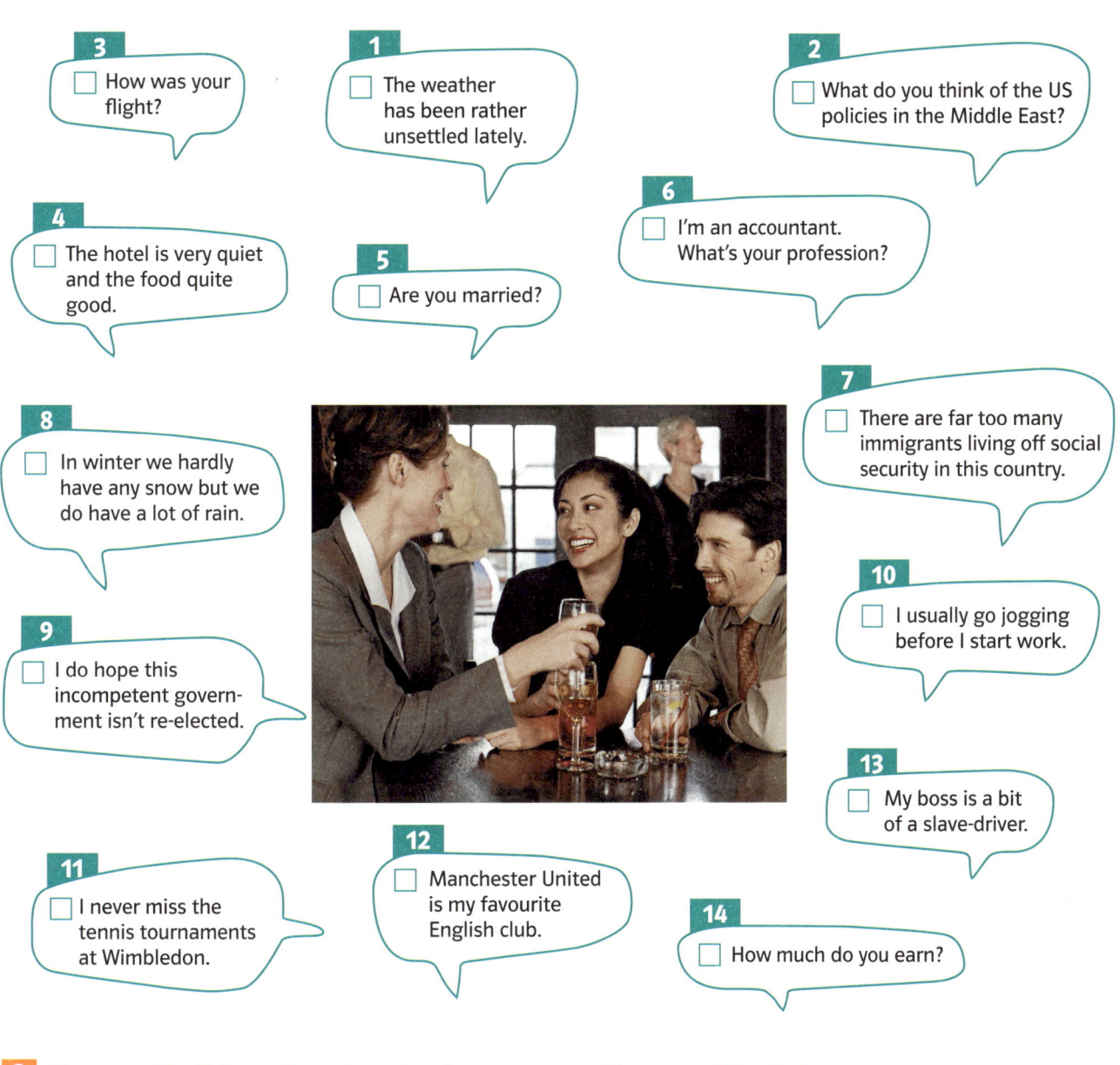

13
☐ My boss is a bit of a slave-driver.

11
☐ I never miss the tennis tournaments at Wimbledon.

12
☐ Manchester United is my favourite English club.

14
☐ How much do you earn?

3 Listen to this dialogue that takes place in a restaurant. Note especially the "spontaneous
◎ A 3.2 will-futures" (for example, "I'll"). Then decide if the following statements are TRUE or FALSE.

	TRUE	FALSE
1. The woman orders a glass of white wine.	☐	☐
2. She is not very polite.	☐	☐
3. The man orders a still mineral water.	☐	☐
4. She orders sardines as her main course.	☐	☐
5. He orders pork as his main course.	☐	☐
6. She orders apple crumble as her dessert.	☐	☐

social security – Sozialhilfe

Grammar refresher

Language and grammar: Future tenses

Tipp: Im Englischen muss Zukünftiges durch eine der *Future tenses* ausgedrückt werden. Im Deutschen wird dagegen vielfach das Präsens verwendet.
I'll call you tomorrow. = Ich rufe Sie morgen an.
Zeitbestimmungen (z. B. *tomorrow, next week, next Friday, in future, in 2020*), verlangen eine der Zukunftsformen des Englischen, ebenso wie manche Verben, die in die Zukunft weisen können (z. B. *to be afraid, to expect, to hope, to promise*).

1. **Will-future**

   Die *Will-future* wird durch *will* + Infinitiv gebildet *(He will come.)*. In der 1. Person Singular und Plural findet man statt *will* gelegentlich *shall (We shall / will be glad to help you.)*. Die *Will-future* wird verwendet:

   a) in **geschäftlicher Korrespondenz** und **förmlichen Berichten**.
      The report will be finished next week.
      We hope the goods will reach you in good condition.
      We are afraid we will be unable to help you any further.
      The training course will start on 1 February.

   b) bei **spontanen Entscheidungen / Absichtsäußerungen** und **Einfällen**.
      How can I possibly reduce my expenditure? I know, I'll sell the car.
      It's a pity he's out. I'll give him a ring later.

2. **Going to-future**

   Die *Going to-future* wird mit *going to* + Infinitiv gebildet *(He is going to ring.)*. Diese Form drückt aus:

   a) eine **überlegte Absicht** des Sprechenden.
      I've decided I'm going to take Bob out to a restaurant. I don't want to cook.
      What are you going to do with these old books? = Was willst du mit diesen alten Büchern machen?
      I'm going to apply for a new job. I've been thinking about it for some time.

   b) eine **hohe Wahrscheinlichkeit**.
      The forecast says it's going to rain on Sunday.
      That driver's going to have an accident if he doesn't watch out.
      (Es kann nicht ausbleiben.)

3. **Present continuous**

   Die Verlaufsform der Gegenwart *(He is coming.)* drückt eine **Vereinbarung** oder **Verabredung** aus, d.h. mehr als eine bloße Absicht.
   They are going to York for the weekend. (Sie haben bereits ein Hotel gebucht.)
   I'm meeting James at the station at 5 pm. (Eine Verabredung und James weiß davon.)
   I'm going to meet Tom at the pub. (Meine Absicht, möglicherweise weiß Tom nichts davon.)

   Abweichend von dieser Regel wird in **Nebensätzen der Zeit** das Präsens (nicht Futur) verwendet.
   I'll let you know when she arrives.
   I'll ring you as soon as I get back to the office.
   You will have to explain that to the clients before they place their orders.

1 Put in the correct tense of the verbs in brackets.

1. We _____ (**dispatch**) the goods next Monday.

2. I _____ (**fly**) to Edinburgh tomorrow. Tina has just booked the flight.

3. I _____ (**pick up**/**you**) at the airport if you like.

4. We expect that prices _____ (**rise**) before Christmas.

5. We _____ (**lose**) market share as soon as we _____ (**put up**) our prices.

6. The export manager _____ (**take**) Mr Chang out for lunch on Tuesday. Mr Chang has accepted.

7. The bar has a new owner. Hopefully the service _____ (**improve**).

8. I _____ (**send**) you an e-mail to confirm your order.

9. You _____ (**receive**) further instructions before you _____ (**start**) the course.

10. I _____ (**try**) again later. The number's engaged.

11. I _____ (**take**) part in the course next month. I've already enrolled.

12. We _____ (**inform**) you as soon as we _____ (**hear**) from him.

2 Translate the sentences with the help of the words in brackets.

1. Die Ware *(goods)* wird am 25. September abgeschickt *(dispatch)*.

   _____

2. Wir hoffen, dass Sie mit den Zahlungsbedingungen *(terms of payment)* einverstanden sind *(agree)*.

   _____

   _____

3. Nächste Woche finden hier drei große Veranstaltungen *(events)* statt *(take place)*.

   _____

   _____

4. Wir gehen davon aus *(trust)*, dass diese Vereinbarung *(agreement)* Ihre Zustimmung findet *(find approval)*.

   _____

   _____

5. In Zukunft werden wir Ihre Anweisungen *(instructions)* genau einhalten *(observe carefully)*.

   _____

   _____

6. Was wirst du machen, nachdem du deine Ausbildung abgeschlossen hast *(complete)*?

   _____

   _____

Phrases refresher

1 Decide which of the alternatives are correct and underline them.

1. **Would you like/Do you want** to see something of Ulm?
2. Mrs Hamilton is still in a meeting. She will be **there/with you** in a few minutes.
3. Please take **place/a seat**.
4. **Take/Drive with** the lift to the third floor. Mr Cameron's office is on the **right/right hand** side.
5. No meat for me, please. I'm **vegetarian/a vegetarian**.
6. We've had a lot of snow **in the last time/lately**.
7. It tastes a bit **like/after** strawberries.
8. I am going to **renounce/do without** a dessert.

2 Find the English equivalents to these expressions which should not be translated literally.

1. Darf ich Ihnen etwas anbieten?

   _____

2. Möchten Sie in Stuttgart etwas besichtigen?

   _____

3. Fahren Sie geradeaus bis zum Kreisverkehr.

   _____

4. Wir möchten Ihnen unsere Firma auf einem Rundgang zeigen.

   _____

5. Wir sollten jetzt lieber zum Parkplatz zurückgehen.

   _____

6. Hier ist die Speisekarte. Wie ist es mit Ihnen? Was nehmen Sie?

   _____

   _____

7. Ich nehme einen Salat als Vorspeise.

   _____

   _____

8. Ich esse lieber Fisch als Fleisch.

   _____

   _____

9. Leider bin ich schon satt.

   _____

   _____

10. Ich hätte lieber ein Eis als Nachtisch.

   _____

   _____

Unit refresher

1 Decide which sector of industry the companies belong to and put them in the table below.

N E R V O Pharmaceuticals

SCOTTISH CHEMICAL PRODUCTS

North Sea Fisheries

Staffordshire Chinaware

MAYFAIR EXCLUSIVE FURNITURE

Vogue **Designer Jeans**

Quickmove Transports

South African Mining Pty

ANG *Management Consultants*

Securitas Insurance Group

St John's Hospital +

Royal Bank of Gibraltar

Radcliffe Stacey & Partners Solicitors

Henderson Machine Tools

Primary sector	Secondary sector	Tertiary sector
Extractive industries → take resources from the land or the sea (e.g. mining, farming, fishing)	Manufacturing industries → make something (e.g. car making or house building)	Services industries → provide services to others (e.g. insurance, education)
_____	_____	_____
_____	_____	_____
_____	_____	_____
_____	_____	_____
_____	_____	_____
_____	_____	_____
_____	_____	_____
_____	_____	_____

solicitor – Anwalt, Anwältin

2 Read the texts (A–E) and find out what products or services the companies offer. It is not important for you to understand every single word – the main thing is to get the general sense. Then complete the texts with the words from the box. Use a dictionary, if necessary.

Caterers • catering • courses • energy • flexibility • goods • individuals • language school • model • office chair • positions • programmes • time • transport company • washing machine

A

Our high-back _____ with 5 star base and fixed arms is adjustable in height and can be locked in seven _____ for reclining support. The seat is wide with 490 x 450 mm. The executive model features genuine leather and hardwood arms. Price: Euro 359.00. The same _____ is also available in black or burgundy easy-care vinyl at Euro 285.00.

B

The _____ offers 3-week _____ for groups. These courses are especially designed to improve the English of staff sent by companies from the continent. Customised one-to-one lessons for executives can be arranged at any _____.

C

Freestanding _____ with extra large drum up to 8 kg. Uses 20% less _____ and water than a standard A-rated model. LC display with programme and temperature selection. Fifteen _____, including two memory programmes. Maximum spin speed: 1400.

D

Transspeed is a _____ with five offices based throughout the UK and a further 125 offices and agents located worldwide. In the ever changing world of today's market places, _____ is a must. The safe and timely transportation of _____ ensures continued profitable growth.

E

Nottingham _____ is a long established business offering _____ services to clients throughout Nottingham. The company provides both businesses and _____ with exactly the right food dependant on the type of budget available. Delivery is free.

3 Listen to two people, who have just met, discussing their companies.
A 3.3 Are the following statements TRUE or FALSE?

	TRUE	FALSE
1. Jonathan's company has 25,000 employees in 13 countries.	☐	☐
2. His company produces automotive components.	☐	☐
3. He often goes bowling with colleagues after work.	☐	☐
4. Laila would prefer to work in a big company.	☐	☐
5. Jonathan's company offers good prospects of promotion.	☐	☐
6. He would like to work abroad if he gets the chance.	☐	☐
7. Laila regularly works out at a fitness centre.	☐	☐
8. Laila is a vegetarian.	☐	☐
9. Jonathan would like to take Laila to a discothèque.	☐	☐

Grammar refresher

Language and grammar: Present perfect or Simple past

Welche Zeitform zu verwenden ist, wird durch den **Zeitraum** bestimmt, in dem die Handlung stattfand: er ist entweder **offen** (d. h. kein Zeitraum wird angegeben oder angedeutet), **abgeschlossen** oder **nicht abgeschlossen**.

Zeitraum offen: I've bought a new jacket. Keine Zeitangabe / offener Zeitraum.
→ **Present perfect**
Zeitraum nicht abgeschlossen: He has written a new play this year. Mit Zeitangabe, wie z. B. *today, this week, just, not yet, this year*. → **Present perfect**

Zeitraum abgeschlossen / angegeben: I bought it last weekend. Zeitraum abgeschlossen / mit Zeitangabe, wie z. B. *yesterday, last year, three weeks ago, in the year 1971, the other day, during.* → **Simple past**
Zeitraum abgeschlossen / angedeutet: Shakespeare wrote many plays.
Er ist tot, daher Zeitraum abgeschlossen. → **Simple past**
I bought the jacket in Oxford Street. Keine Zeitangabe, aber häufig Ortsangabe, die zeigt, dass der Zeitraum abgeschlossen sein muss. → **Simple past**.

automotive components – Bauteile für die Automobilindustrie

Present perfect

1. *Present perfect* wird für Vorgänge verwendet, die in der Vergangenheit anfingen und **bis in die Gegenwart andauern** (d. h. Zeitraum ist nicht abgeschlossen).
She has been unemployed until now. = Sie war bis jetzt arbeitslos.
He has been working here since 2001. = Er arbeitet hier seit 2001.

2. *Present perfect* wird bei Vorgängen verwendet, die in der Vergangenheit stattfanden, wenn die **Auswirkungen in der Gegenwart von Bedeutung sind** und der Zeitraum nicht angegeben (d. h. offen) ist.
I've lost my umbrella. (Er fehlt mir immer noch, da keine Zeitangabe.)
We have received your report of 12 May. (Wann der Bericht eintraf ist offen, wichtig ist, dass er vorliegt.)

Simple past

1. *Simple past* wird für Vorgänge verwendet, die während eines angegebenen oder angedeuteten **Zeitraums in der Vergangenheit**, der **abgeschlossen** ist, stattfanden.
Last year sales increased by 11 %. (Zeitraum abgeschlossen / angegeben.)
I left my briefcase on the train. (Zeitraum abgeschlossen / angedeutet.)

2. *Simple past* wird für **aufeinanderfolgende Vorgänge der Vergangenheit** verwendet, auch wenn der Zeitraum / Zeitpunkt nicht genannt ist (Zeitraum abgeschlossen / angedeutet). Es ist die Zeitform für Erzählungen, Berichte, etc.
Your service engineer arrived a day late. He did not bring along the necessary forms and forgot to sign the test certificate. We are highly dissatisfied with your service.

Tipp: Das Problem für Deutsche, die Englisch lernen, besteht darin, dass im Englischen *Simple past* bei einem abgeschlossenen Zeitraum unerlässlich ist, auch wenn im Deutschen das Perfekt verwendet wird. **!**
Ich habe ihn gestern getroffen. = I met him yesterday.

---

1 **Put in the correct form of the verbs in brackets.**

1. I _____ (buy) a motorbike. Do you like it?

2. We _____ (see) him yesterday in the cinema.

3. I _____ (receive / just) an e-mail which says when they are going to arrive.

4. I _____ (live) in Tunbridge Wells all my life.

5. That's a nice pullover. When _____ (buy / you) it?

6. We _____ (spend) our holidays in the South of France last year.

7. I _____ (lose) my handbag. I think I _____ (leave) it on the bus.

8. I _____ (work) for this company since 2003.

9. We _____ (move) here in 1995.

10. I _____ (meet) her in town the other day.

11. We _____ (remind / you) twice, on 15 and 30 June.

12. I _____ (never / be) to New Zealand.

2 Translate the following sentences into English.

1. Im vergangenen September haben wir 10 % mehr Kopierer verkauft als im August.

   _____

2. Vor der Messe (*fair*) haben wir uns mit allen Kunden in Verbindung gesetzt (*contact*).

   _____

3. Wir beziehen (*buy*) seit Jahren regelmäßig Ersatzteile (*spare parts*) von dieser Firma.

   _____

4. Unser Umsatz (*turnover*) war noch nie so hoch wie jetzt.

   _____

5. Der Artikel wurde sorgfältig (*carefully*) getestet und hat unser Werk (*plant*) in einwandfreiem Zustand (*in perfect condition*) verlassen.

   _____

   _____

6. Im zweiten Quartal (*quarter*) sind die Preise gefallen.

   _____

7. Dieser Dienst war bis jetzt nicht verfügbar (*available*).

   _____

Phrases refresher

Choose the most suitable adjectives from the box to fill in the gaps. In some cases there are several correct solutions.

> customised • exotic • global • high-quality • leading • legal • long-lasting • major • medium-sized • organic • public • reliable • state-of-the-art • upmarket • well-known

1. We import _____ fruit from South America.
2. The _____ form of our company is a _____ limited company.
3. I work for an _____ advertising agency.
4. We develop _____ software solutions.
5. My company is a _____ food retailer.
6. Our instruments are both _____ and _____ .
7. We are a _____ family firm.
8. They are a _____ manufacturer of machine tools.
9. We are a chain of _____ cosmetics suppliers.
10. Our _____ products are _____ all over the world.

> machine tools – Werkzeugmaschinen

Unit refresher

1 Look at the photos of office supplies and equipment in your student's book and fill in the crossword.

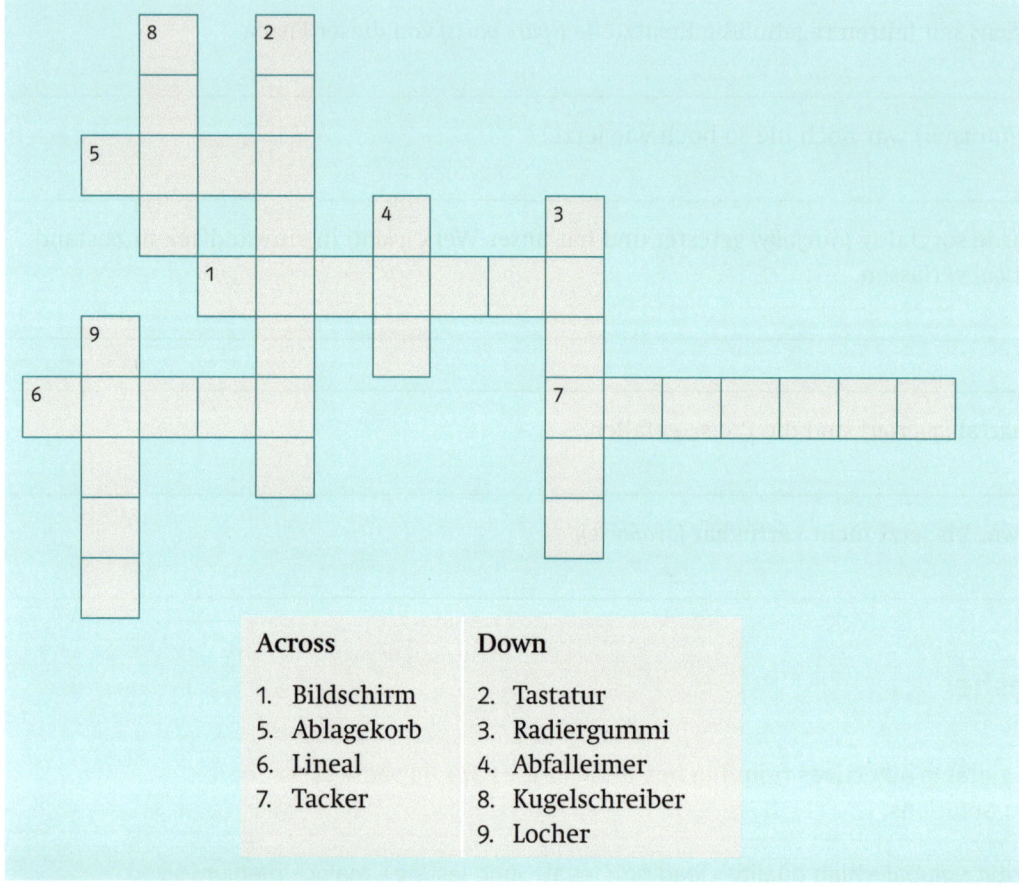

Across

1. Bildschirm
5. Ablagekorb
6. Lineal
7. Tacker

Down

2. Tastatur
3. Radiergummi
4. Abfalleimer
8. Kugelschreiber
9. Locher

2 Match the departments (1.–6.) with the appropriate statements (a.–f.) and draw lines. Use a dictionary, if necessary.

1. Legal Department

2. Domestic Sales

3. Customer Relations

4. Research and Development

5. Quality Assurance

6. Controlling

a. In our department there is no opportunity to speak English. All our customers are located in Germany.

b. What I hate about my present job is all those phone calls from angry customers. What I like about it is when the customers are grateful for my services and tell me so.

c. My department supports the different sections in their operational and strategic planning. It defines future targets and makes appropriate budget forecasts.

d. We ensure that our products and services meet specified requirements. Our aim is to improve work processes and efficiency to make sure that standards of quality are being met.

e. In our fast-changing industry we must continually revise the design and range of our products. We have to anticipate changes in technology and in our customers' needs.

f. All contracts have first to be approved by my boss. She is a lawyer.

3 James has just started at Orion plc and is trying to find out something about the firm from Julian. Listen to their conversation and answer the questions.

A 3.4

1. How did Julian start off in the company?

   _____

   _____

2. Mention two departments Julian has not worked in.

   _____

3. What department are they both working in now?

   _____

4. What foreign language does Julian speak?

   _____

5. What reason does he give for his fluency?

   _____

6. In which European countries does James have relatives?

   _____

7. What do many people think about the canteen?

   _____

Grammar refresher

Language and grammar: Gerund and infinitive

Das *Gerund* hat die gleiche Form wie das Partizip Präsens des Verbs, also die *-ing*-Form (z. B. *writing, coming*). Es ist erforderlich:

1. nach **Präpositionen**, wie *about, after, at, before, by, for, from, in, of, on, to, with, without*.
   Thank you for calling.
   Please check the list before filling in the form.
   We look forward to hearing from you.
   He insisted on seeing the boss.

2. nach bestimmten **Ausdrücken**, wie *it is no use, it is no good, it is worthwhile, would you mind, I / we don't mind, cannot help, can't stand.*
   Would you mind waiting a few minutes?
   It is no use sending another e-mail.

3. nach bestimmten **Verben**, wie *to appreciate, to avoid, to consider, to enjoy, to finish, to imagine, to justify, to involve, to mean, to mention, to postpone, to risk, to stop, to suggest.*
   We would suggest sending the goods by air.
   That means price cutting by at least 20 %.
   The new project will involve working overtime.
   Please stop talking while I'm trying to listen to the news.

Manche Verben verlangen *Gerund* oder **Infinitiv**, je nach Bedeutung, so z. B.:
He continued **talking** about his holidays. (Er spricht weiter darüber.)
He continued **to talk** about his holidays. (Er fängt ein neues Thema an.)
We do not permit **smoking**. (Kein indirektes Objekt genannt.)
We do not permit our workers **to smoke**. (Indirektes Objekt genannt.)
I remember **seeing** him before. (Sprecher blickt zurück.)
I must remember **to ring** him up. (Sprecher blickt nach vorne.)

Nach den meisten Verben folgt im Englischen, wie im Deutschen, der **Infinitiv**.
We hope to hear from you soon.
They failed to read the small print.
He managed to convince his colleagues.
We would now like to inform you of the results.

Tipp: Die unter Punkt 3. genannten Verben, die das *Gerund* nach sich ziehen, kommen in der Geschäftskommunikation jedoch häufig vor, insbesondere das Verb *suggest*, und man muss sich diese einprägen.

!

---

1 Put in the correct form of the verbs in brackets.

1. Thank you for _____ (**draw**) this error to our attention.

2. I suggest _____ (**discuss**) the matter next week.

3. We look forward to _____ (**serve**) you again.

4. We hope _____ (**get**) another order from you soon.

5. They finished _____ (**pack**) at 4 pm.

6. Would you mind _____ (**call**) a technician?

7. We appreciate your _____ (**help**) us in this situation.

8. My boss tends to postpone _____ (take) difficult decisions.

9. We cannot risk _____ (lose) our best customers.

10. We are sure this will not prevent them from _____ (place) an order.

11. You must remember _____ (inform) them of your change of address.

12. She raised the money by _____ (sell) her flat.

13. We would like _____ (assist) you as much as possible.

14. In this particular case I am against _____ (make) a complaint.

15. They suggested _____ (cut) their prices by 10% to win the order.

2 Translate these sentences into English.

1. Wir hoffen bald wieder von Ihnen zu hören.

_____

2. Wir freuen uns darauf, bald wieder von Ihnen zu hören.

_____

3. Es hat keinen Zweck noch länger auf den Anruf zu warten.

_____

4. Wir werden unser Bestes tun, um zu vermeiden unsere Kunden zu verärgern *(annoy)*.

_____

_____

5. Wir sind sehr daran interessiert, auf dem kanadischen Markt Fuß zu fassen *(enter the market)*.

_____

_____

6. Wir müssen darauf bestehen, dass wir unverzüglich *(without delay)* benachrichtigt werden.

_____

_____

7. Ich schlage vor, das Geld einer gemein-
   nützigen Einrichtung *(charity)* zu geben.

   _____

   _____

   _____

   _____

8. Kaufen Sie diesen Artikel nicht, ohne ihn
   mit den anderen zu vergleichen *(compare)*.

   _____

   _____

   _____

   _____

Phrases refresher

1 The second half of several words has been deleted. Complete these words.

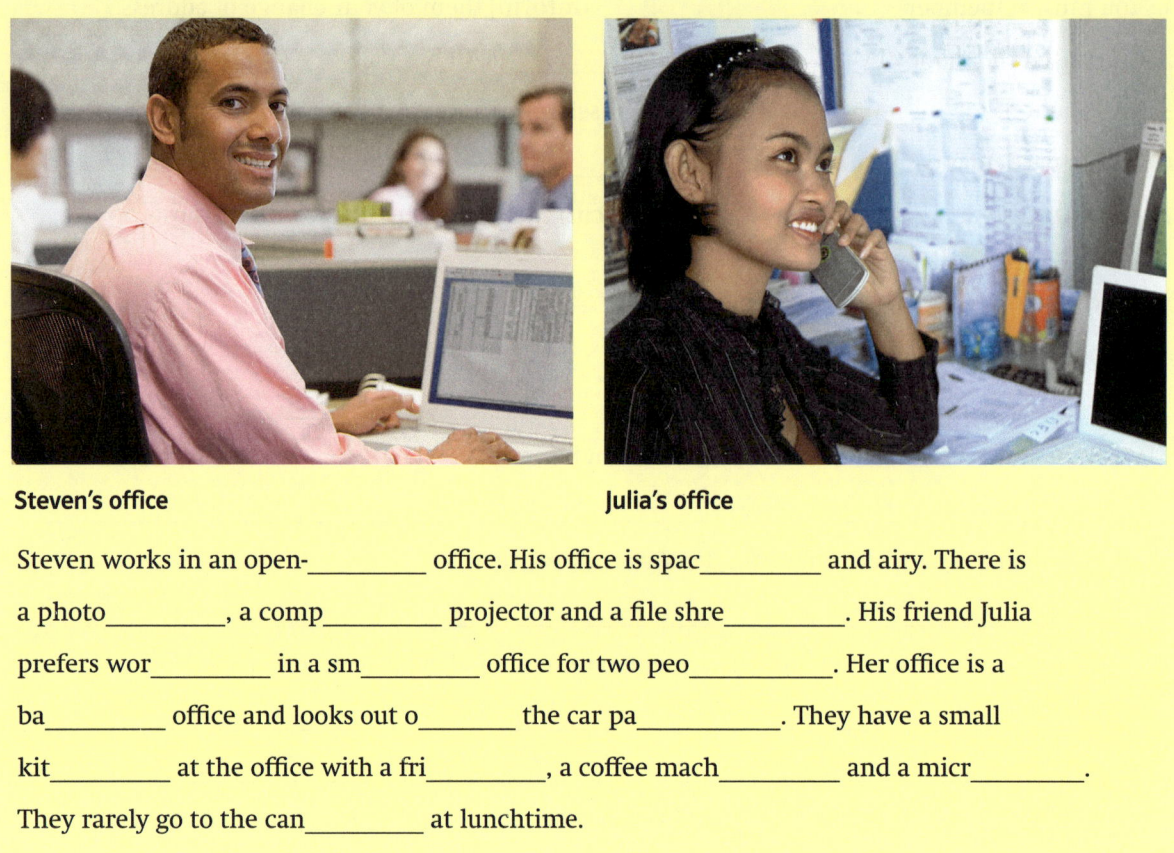

Steven's office   **Julia's office**

Steven works in an open-_____ office. His office is spac_____ and airy. There is

a photo_____, a comp_____ projector and a file shre_____. His friend Julia

prefers wor_____ in a sm_____ office for two peo_____. Her office is a

ba_____ office and looks out o_____ the car pa_____. They have a small

kit_____ at the office with a fri_____, a coffee mach_____ and a micr_____.

They rarely go to the can_____ at lunchtime.

2 Please complete the sentences describing the introduction of colleagues to a new trainee.

"Let me tell you who's who. This is Tarik Massoudi, he **1** _____

(zuständig sein für) exports to North Africa. Thomas Schulz, the export manager, is his

2 _____ **(Vorgesetzter).** That's Fiona Meinhard over there at the

window who **3** _____ **(bearbeiten)** enquiries from Germany.

She **4** _____ **(unterstehen)** the head of department, Leonie

Hansen. The young man with the beard, who has just come in, is Mark Gruber, he

5 _____ **(Sachbearbeiter sein)** purchasing. The young woman in

the smart costume is Maria Schaefer who **6** _____

(sich kümmern um) that bills are paid punctually."

Unit 5 Telephoning

Unit refresher

1 Complete the telephone conversation with the words from the box.

> answering machine • catch • engaged • extension • get • get back • hold • line • message • pass •
> put • repeat • speaking • wrong number

A: Good morning. XYZ plc speaking. How can I help you?

B: Sorry. I didn't quite **1** _____ the name. Could you **2** _____ it?

A: It's XYZ plc.

B: Oh right. I'm sorry, I think I must have got a **3** _____.

A: No problem. Goodbye.

B: Good morning. Is that ABC Components?

C: It is. Jonathan Davidson **4** _____. How can I help you?

B: I'd like to speak to Martha Johnson-Webb, please.

C: Certainly. I'll try to **5** _____ you through to her **6** _____. […]
I'm afraid the line's **7** _____. Would you like to **8** _____ or shall I ask
her to ring you back?

B: Could I possibly leave a **9** _____?

C: Certainly. What shall I tell her? I didn't **10** _____ your name.

B: Oh sorry. I'm Peter Jones from Ace Ads. I need to talk to her about the new advertising campaign.
I suggest a meeting tomorrow or Friday. Please ask her to leave a message on my
11 _____. I'll **12** _____ to her tomorrow.

C: OK. I'll **13** _____ the message on to her as soon as her **14** _____ is free.

B: It is rather important. Thank you very much. Goodbye.

2 Write out the following text messages in full.

> TXS FOR YR MSG. IMO YR WRK
> IS XLENT. BTHW RUCMNG 2NITE?
> CULBR. RGDS SARAH

1. _____
_____
_____

> FYI: AFAIK NO1 IS AVAILABLE
> 2DAY. SRY. 2MORO WOULD
> PROLLY BE BETTER.
> ATB JAMES

2. _____
_____
_____

> RUOK?
> PCM ASAP. I WAN2 START EARLY
> AND FINISH THE WRK IN TIME.
> RGDS CAROLINE

3. _____
_____
_____

3 Listen to this conversation between Sarah and her aunt Emily, who has a small interior
◎ A3.5 design business. Then answer the questions.

1. How did you let people know you were going to be late before mobile phones became available?

_____

2. What does Sarah think is the purpose of networking?

_____

3. What other applications does she use?

_____

4. What is the main advantage of the mobile phone as far as Emily is concerned?

_____

5. What kind of a company does Emily's friend Roger have?

_____

6. How many people does he employ?

_____

Grammar refresher

Language and grammar: Passive voice

Das Passiv wird mithilfe des Partizips Perfekt und der entsprechenden Form von
to be gebildet. Der Urheber wird im Deutschen mit „von" angeschlossen, im
Englischen mit *by*.

aktiv	passiv
Tim repaired the defect.	The defect was repaired by Tim.
They will publish their report soon.	Their report will soon be published.

Bei einem **im Gang befindlichen Prozess** wird die **Verlaufsform** benutzt.
All our machines are being serviced at the moment.
The parts were being taken there by a lorry when the accident happened.

Das Passiv wird im Englischen häufiger verwendet als im Deutschen:
1. zur **Betonung** durch Umstellung an den Satzanfang.

aktiv	passiv
We will process your order.	Your order will be processed.
(Betonung auf *We*.)	(Betonung auf *Your order*.)
You must complete the report by 2 pm.	The report must be completed by
(Betonung auf *You*.)	2 pm. (Betonung auf *The report*.)

2. zur Wiedergabe von „man".

Man wird ihn bestrafen.	He will be punished.
Man gewährte uns keinerlei Rabatt.	We were not granted any discount.
Kann man sich auf ihn verlassen?	Can he be relied on?

3. wenn der **Urheber unbekannt / unspezifisch** ist (z. B. *nobody, people, one*).
    My briefcase was stolen. (I don't know by whom.)
    An IT specialist was sent for.

> **Tipp:** Im Deutschen werden beim Passiv bisweilen „werden" oder „worden" weg-
> gelassen – dies führt leicht zu Missverständnissen im Englischen.
> Der Stuhl ist repariert (worden). = The chair has been repaired. (Es ist geschehen.)
> Der Stuhl wird repariert. = The chair is being repaired. (Es geschieht gerade.)
> Der Stuhl wird repariert (werden). = The chair will be repaired. (Es wird geschehen.)

!

1 Delete the incorrect alternatives.

1. Our goods are always **packed/being packed** in sturdy containers.
2. He was **invited/being invited** to an interview last Friday.
3. A new product is **launched/being launched** on the market at the present time.
4. He was **chosen/being chosen** to show the guests round the factory.
5. This product is **updated/being updated** at the moment.

2 Put in the correct form of the verbs in brackets (sometimes more than one form is possible).

1. The annual meeting _____ (**hold**) next week.

2. The plans _____ (**steal**) last Monday.

3. A product can _____ (**call**) by different names in different countries.

4. Our exhibition stand _____ (**always design**) by an outside company.

5. The spare parts _____ (**send**) by courier as soon as possible.

6. Our customers _____ (**always treat**) in a friendly manner.

7. The visitors _____ (**pick up**) at the airport tomorrow.

8. Two working days _____ (**lose**) this year due to the weather.

9. Over 50 million euros _____ (**spend**) on advertising last year.

10. Normally, their brochures _____ (**print**) on acid-free paper.

11. I am glad that Mr Palmer _____ (**appoint**) sales manger.

12. All the employees _____ (**tell**) at the meeting last night that
    they would get a bonus.

3 Translate this excerpt from a company brochure into English. Then use your translation
as the basis for a reply to a complaint about one of the watches and describe how the
customer's watch was tested before it left the works.

Bevor unsere Uhren *(watches)* das Werk *(works)* verlassen, werden sie
eingehend *(thoroughly)* geprüft. Sie werden ins Wasser getaucht *(submerge
in)*, um sicherzugehen *(make sure)*, dass sie wasserdicht *(waterproof)* sind.
Aus einer Höhe von einem Meter werden sie auf einen Hartholzboden *(hardwood floor)* geworfen *(drop on)* und danach werden alle Funktionen über-
prüft *(examine)*. Schließlich wird die Oberfläche *(surface)* auf winzige
(minute) Kratzer *(scratches)* untersucht *(inspect for)*. Verpackt werden die
Uhren in Etuis *(cases)* aus Metall mit Schaumstoffeinlage *(foam moulding)*.

Phrases refresher

1 Fill in the missing verbs from the box.

access • agree • appreciate • give • hold • make sure • say • settle • speak • tell

1. Please _____ that she gets the message immediately.

2. I'm afraid we cannot _____ to this proposal.

3. Would you prefer to _____ or shall I ask her to ring you back?

4. Could you _____ me his extension, please?

5. I'm afraid I can't _____ the file on my computer.

6. I wish to _____ the matter now.

7. I really need to _____ to the export manager

8. I would really _____ it if you told him that.

9. Could you please _____ him that I rang?

10. I can only _____ that I am sorry.

2 Find the English equivalents to these telephone expressions.

1. Kann ich ihm etwas ausrichten?

   _____

2. Könnten Sie den Namen bitte buchstabieren?

   _____

3. Könnten Sie mich mit Mrs Fraser verbinden?

   _____

4. Ich werde mich selbst darum kümmern.

   _____

   _____

5. Leider weiß ich über diesen Auftrag nicht Bescheid.

   _____

   _____

6. Vielen Dank für Ihr Verständnis.

   _____

   _____

7. Das ist überaus bedauerlich.

   _____

   _____

Unit 6 Making arrangements

Unit refresher

1 Ihr schwedischer Chef ist zur Zeit in Urlaub, aber Sie haben inzwischen für seine nächste Geschäftsreise die nachstehend angegebenen Flüge gebucht. Ferner haben Sie für den 9. bis 16. März ein Einzelzimmer im Royal Toronto Hotel (100 Front Street W, Toronto, Ontario, M5J 1E3, www.royaltoronto@p-hotels.com) reservieren lassen. Schreiben Sie Ihrem Chef eine E-Mail in Englisch (b.oddson@intchem.com), um ihm alles Wichtige mitzuteilen.

Date	Departure	Arrival	Flight	Duration	Cabin	Status
Tue 9 Mar	11:50 Munich	14:40 Toronto	LH9636 Operated by Air Canada	8h50	Business	✓
Tue 16 Mar	20:05 Toronto	10:05 +1 Munich	LH9637 Operated by Air Canada	8h00	Business	✓

+ 1 Arrives the following day.   ✓ Indicates that the airline has confirmed your request.

Whether you're here for a meeting or to relax, this landmark hotel "at the center of it all" has everything you need. Luxurious surroundings, refined guest rooms and suites, and a fully-stocked Business Center – The Royal Toronto Hotel is the ultimate downtown Toronto hotel.

about us | back

Royal Toronto Hotel

2 ◎ A 3.6   Jane Fawkes has been asked to organise a visit to Brighton Pavilion, a former royal palace, and lunch at the Grand Hotel for a delegation of Chinese businessmen. She rings the Brighton Pavilion. Listen to the dialogue and answer the following questions.

1. How big is the Chinese delegation?
   _____

2. What time does Jane Fawkes book the tour for?
   _____

3. Why does Jane Fawkes think it would be a good idea to have a Chinese interpreter?
   _____

4. How long roughly does the tour take?
   _____

5. How are the Chinese being transported from place to place?
   _____

6. What time is lunch scheduled for?
   _____

7. How much does admission and the guided tour cost in total?
   _____

3 Study the text on taking the minutes in your student's book. Then tick (✓) whether the following statements are TRUE or FALSE.

	TRUE	FALSE
1. The minutes are a written record of the transactions of a meeting.	☐	☐
2. Minutes are not accepted as evidence in court.	☐	☐
3. Apologies for non-attendance are read out but not recorded.	☐	☐
4. It is not essential to keep a word for word account of any discussion.	☐	☐
5. The participants cannot make corrections later on.	☐	☐

Grammar refresher

Language and grammar: Continuous form and Simple form

Die Wahl der Zeitform wird durch die **Art der Handlung / des Vorgangs** bestimmt.

Continuous form (Verlaufsform)
Sie wird gebildet mit *to be* und der *-ing*-Form des Verbs und beschreibt:
1. eine Handlung, die gerade vor sich geht. He is checking his e-mails. She was leaving the office when the phone rang.
2. eine prozessartige Entwicklung. Inflation has been going up for years.
3. eine Vereinbarung / Verabredung. They are leaving for India on Sunday. (Der Flug ist schon gebucht.)

Oft signalisiert die *Continuous form*, dass etwas vorübergehend ist.
She is living with her parents. (Vielleicht zieht sie bald aus.)
She lives with her parents. (Kein Hinweis, dass der Zustand vorübergehend ist.)
Signalwörter sind z. B. *at the moment, in the last few days, just, now, still, when, for (five years), since (2009)*.

Simple form (Grundform)
Sie wird verwendet bei:
1. Vorgängen / Handlungen ohne Zeitbezug. He reads novels. The Rhine flows into the North Sea.
2. wiederholten Handlungen. He travels to work by bus every day.
   Signalwörter sind z. B. *always, ever, every (day), generally, never, normally, often, rarely, regularly, sometimes*.
3. kurzen Handlungen / Vorgängen. The phone rang (kurze Handlung) when I was writing the report (längere Handlung).

Bei einigen Verben, die keine aktive Handlung ausdrücken, kommt die *Continuous form* fast nie vor, z. B. *forget, know, hear, own, possess, remember, seem, understand, want, wish, want*.
I can hear the traffic. (unfreiwillig)   He is listening to music. (freiwillig)

Tipp: Da es in der deutschen Schriftsprache keine Verlaufsform gibt, muss man im Englischen darauf achten, gerade vor sich gehende Handlungen und prozessartige Entwicklungen in der *Continuous form* wiederzugeben.
Andererseits muss man bedenken, dass man im Englischen mit der *Simple form* oft eine Gewohnheit, etwas Allgemeingültiges oder Wiederholtes zum Ausdruck bringt und nicht etwas gerade vor sich Gehendes oder Vorübergehendes.

!

1 Put in the correct form of the verbs in brackets.

1. When we landed in Tenerife the sun _____ (shine).

2. They always _____ (stay) at the Palace Hotel.

3. Petrol prices _____ (rise) before long weekends.

4. Normally, we _____ (not grant) any discounts.

5. At the moment there are signs that the situation _____ (improve).

6. They _____ (wait) here for more than an hour.

7. I _____ (remember/clearly) the incident at the conference.

8. Most children _____ (love) sweets and _____ (hate) spinach.

9. We _____ (recycle/regularly) cardboard and paper.

10. Until now they _____ (produce/never) anything of such poor quality.

11. As an attachment we _____ (send) you our pricelist.

12. I _____ (clean) the office when the postman

    _____ (arrive).

2 Please translate the following sentences into English.

1. Miss Johnson wartet an der Rezeption auf Sie.

    _____

2. Leider haben wir die Überweisung *(remittance)* bis heute noch nicht erhalten.

    _____

3. Er spricht Englisch und lernt gerade Französisch.

    _____

4. Wir versenden *(dispatch)* pro Woche etwa 150 Kataloge *(brochures)*.

    _____

5. Dieses Haus gehört uns nicht.

    _____

6. Es regnet jetzt schon die ganze Woche.

    _____

7. Im Winter regnet es in Schottland sehr viel.

    _____

8. Die Lage auf dem Arbeitsmarkt *(job market)* wird immer *(more and more)* schwieriger.

    _____

    _____

9. Ich suche dieses Muster *(pattern)* seit Wochen und nun habe ich es endlich gefunden.

    _____

    _____

Phrases refresher

1 **Choose the correct words from the box to fill in the gaps.**

adjourn • aisle • cancel • conference room • diary • display • ensuite bathroom • floor space • is chairing • surcharge

1. Please reserve an ___aisle___ seat on the flight to Boston.

2. Is there a _____ for the intercity to Manchester?

3. We require a single room with ___ensuite___.

4. We need a ___conf room___ to seat 15 people.

5. We regret that we have to ___cancel___ the booking.

6. My _____ is full, I'm afraid.

7. He _____ the meeting next Monday.

8. We shall _____ for lunch at 12:30.

9. We would like to _____ our handbags at the Luggage Fair.

10. We wish to reserve _____ for a small stand.

2 **Find the English equivalents to these expressions which should not be translated literally, i.e. word for word.**

1. Erster oder zweiter Klasse? Einfach oder hin und zurück?

   _____

   _____

2. Leider muss ich die Reservierung stornieren.

   _____

   _____

3. Ich bin mir dessen bewusst, dass dies sehr kurzfristig geschieht.

   _____

   _____

4. Donnerstag würde mir gut passen und am Freitag geht es bei mir den ganzen Tag.

   _____

   _____

5. Gibt es noch Wortmeldungen? Sollen wir jetzt abstimmen?

   _____

6. Der Vorsitzende gibt sich die Ehre, Sie zu einem Empfang im Palace Hotel einzuladen.

   _____

   _____

Unit 7 Making presentations

Unit refresher

1 A gremlin has jumbled these compound terms. Study the text on preparing and delivering a presentation in your student's book and sort them out.

overhead cards

computer language

prompt aids

eye transparencies

flip projector

visual chart

powerpoint contact

body slides

1. computer _____

2. body _____

3. flip _____

4. eye _____

5. powerpoint _____

6. visual _____

7. overhead _____

8. prompt _____

2
A 3.7
Ms Joanna Woodhouse from the PR department of the fashion company Zing plc is interviewed by Eric Dowling, a journalist from the local radio. Listen to their dialogue and answer the questions.

1. What happened to sales in January?

_____
_____

2. What reason does Ms Woodhouse give for this development?

_____
_____

3. What were sales like in February and March?

_____
_____

4. How important are online sales for the company?

_____

5. What general trend in retailing does Ms Woodhouse mention?

_____

6. How high were sales in May and June?

_____

7. What happened to sales in August?

_____

gremlin – Kobold

3 Study the following text and insert the names of the countries to complete the bar chart showing the ranking of Germany's ten most important export partners.

In the year under review, The Netherlands were Germany's second most important export partner, closely followed by the USA and the UK. Switzerland was in the last place but one among Germany's top ten export partners. Exports to Poland amounted to a total of 31,626 million euros. Austria imported more than Belgium but less than Italy. Apart from the USA only one other non-European country was among Germany's main export partners, namely the People's Republic of China which imported more from Germany than Switzerland but less than Belgium which was in seventh place. France imported goods worth a record sum of 81,941 million euros.

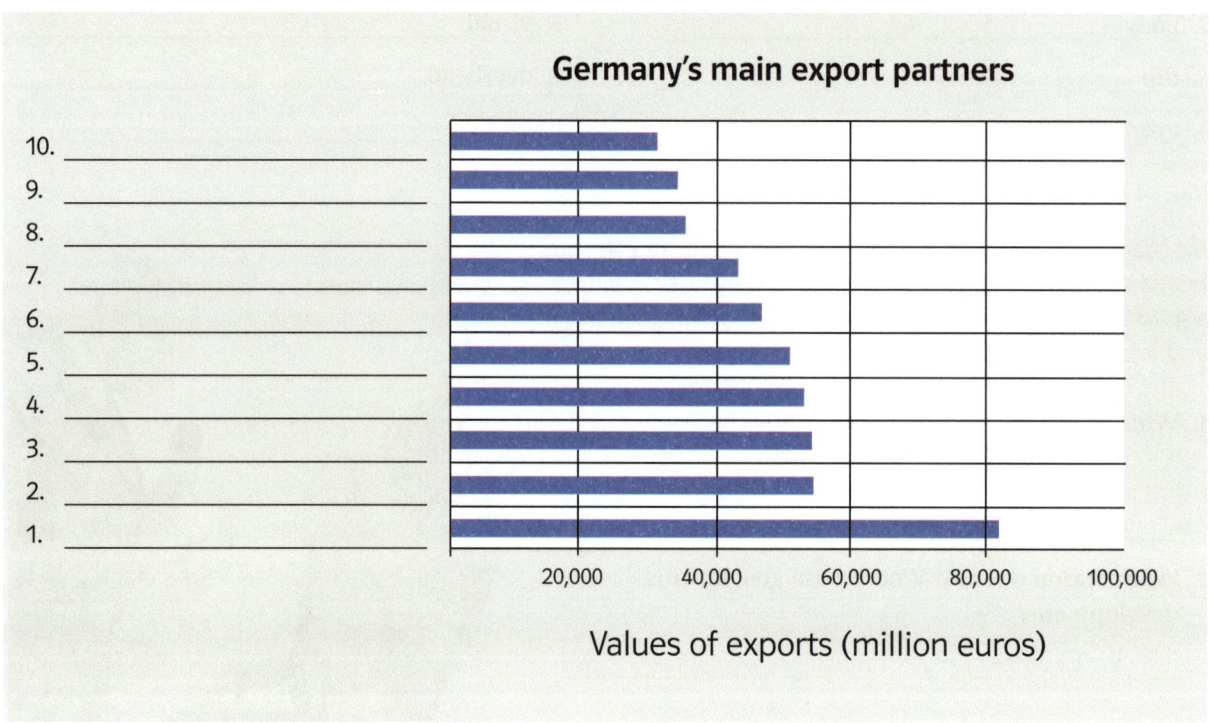

Germany's main export partners

10. _____

9. _____

8. _____

7. _____

6. _____

5. _____

4. _____

3. _____

2. _____

1. _____

20,000   40,000   60,000   80,000   100,000

Values of exports (million euros)

4 Describe the movements of the arrows.

Example: to rise / go up / increase sharply

1. _____

2. _____

3. _____

4. _____

5. _____

6. _____

Grammar refresher

Language and grammar: Numbers

Hundred, thousand, million, billion
Tausender werden im Englischen **durch Komma abgetrennt, Hunderter** (Dezimal-stelle) **durch Punkt,** genau umgekehrt wie im Deutschen.
The total invoice amount is GBP 12,345,678.90
Vor *hundred, thousand, million, billion* steht der unbestimmte Artikel oder eine Zahl.
Some insects travel a / one hundred miles or more.
Million (abgekürzt *m*) und *billion* (abgekürzt *bn*) **als Teil einer Zahl sind unveränder-lich**, anders als im Deutschen.
Iceland's gross domestic product (GDP) is estimated at 12 billion US dollars.
At present the EU has about 500 million inhabitants.
Aber: Millions of people have applied for a Green Card.
Wichtig: million (m) = Million (Mio.); billion (bn) = a thousand million = Milliarde (Mrd.) **!**

Wiederholungszahlen
once = einmal, **twice** = zweimal, **three times** = dreimal, **four times** = viermal, usw.
In April there was five times as much rain as in the same month last year.

Bruchzahlen
½ = a / one half = die / eine Hälfte
Substantive werden mit *of*, **Maße und Mengen mit** *a* **angeschlossen.**
One third of the passengers walked **half a** mile to the bus terminal. It took them one and a half hours. **Achtung:** Vor *half* steht kein *the*.
He was promised **half** of the profit. (= ... **die** Hälfte des Gewinns)
⅓ = a / one third, ¼ = a fourth / quarter, ⅕ = a fifth, ⅙ = a sixth, usw.
¾ = three quarter**s**. **Der Nenner einer Bruchzahl steht im Plural.**
They finally managed to repay four fifths of the sum in question.

Prozentzahlen
Das **Prozentzeichen** wird **ohne Zwischenraum** angehängt.
25 % = 25 per cent = one quarter. **Achtung:** one out of / in seven = jeder siebente; **!**
seven out of ten = sieben von zehn = 70 Prozent
One in five men said he had heard of the brand, that is 20 % of those interviewed.

---

1 Complete the sentences by translating the expressions in brackets into English.
Use commas and points as in English.

1. In February we sold **(7456230)** _____ units, that is **(2,5 Prozent)**
_____ more than in January.

2. This year for the first time their turnover was more than **(eine Milliarde Pfund)** _____.

3. We've already reminded them **(zweimal)** _____.

4. **(Sieben von zehn)** _____ of those interviewed said they use online banking.

5. He owned **(die Hälfte)** _____ of the company's shares.

6. **(Millionen)** _____ of people had their flights cancelled.

7. We had to walk at least **(eine halbe Meile)** _____ to our hotel.

gross domestic product (GDP) – Bruttoinlandsprodukt (BIP)

2 Please translate the text into English.

Die Europäische Union will mit ihrer Agenda 2020 die Wirtschaftskrise überwinden *(overcome)*. Die Beschäftigungsquote *(employment rate)* soll *(is to rise)* von 69 Prozent auf drei Viertel der erwerbsfähigen *(employable)* Bevölkerung steigen.

Teil der Agenda ist das Klimapaket *(climate package)*, demzufolge *(under which)* der Anteil erneuerbarer *(renewable)* Energien auf ein Fünftel erhöht werden soll.

Die Quote der Schulabbrecher *(school drop out rate)* beträgt in der EU derzeit 15 Prozent; sie soll auf unter 10 Prozent verringert werden. Bis *(By)* 2020 sollen vier von zehn EU-Bürgern einen akademischen Abschluss *(academic degree)* haben.

Die Zahl der Menschen, deren Einkommen weniger als 60 Prozent des Durchschnittseinkommens *(average income)* ihres Landes beträgt, soll um 20 Millionen sinken.

Phrases refresher

1 Delete the incorrect alternatives.

1. Has everyone **received**/**become** a copy of the handout?
2. I should like to start by **saying**/**telling** you something about my company.
3. I intend to **hold**/**keep** my presentation as brief as possible.
4. My presentation will **handle**/**deal** with …
5. I would **welcome**/**greet** any questions at the end of my presentation.
6. I should like to finish by **telling**/**saying** that …

2 Put in the correct words from the box.

connection • example • gist • handout • overview • point • questions • statistics • trend

1. An excellent _____ of this is …

2. The _____ of the matter is …

3. A _____ emerges from these figures.

4. In this _____ it is worth mentioning …

5. Let me give you some basic _____.

6. The handout gives an _____ of the relevant figures and statistics.

7. Now my second _____ is …

8. I will refer to the _____ as I go along.

9. I would welcome any _____ at the end of my presentation.

Unit 8 Form of written communication

Unit refresher

1 There are seven mistakes in the e-mail below. Find and correct them.

From: f.wolff@arco-bauelemente.de
To: james.palmer@engineering-consulting.co.uk
sent: 201_-10-15
Subject: Electronica Fair in Munich, 9–12 November

dear James

thank you for suggesting that we meet at the Electronica Fair in Munich next month to discuss class 3 certification by british Certification authorities. I'll be in Munich for two days only. Could we meet on 10 November at 9 am or on 11 November at 2 pm at our stand in hall 2?

yours faithfully

Franz Wolff
Messrs Arco Bauelemente GbR
Stahlstr. 127
42657 Solingen
Tel. +49 212 815720
Fax +49 212 815721
www.arco-bauelemente.de

2 Listen to this conversation between three professionals and answer the questions.

A 3.8

1. What is the first advantage of e-mails that Tristan mentions?

   _____

2. Why does Sarah's firm send letters?

   _____

3. What is the one big drawback with e-mails?

   _____

4. Why does Sarah's firm also send faxes?

   _____

   _____

5. What is the great advantage of e-mails that Andrew mentions?

   _____

   _____

6. When should you not send off an e-mail?

   _____

   _____

3 Insert the jumbled elements on the next page into the letter form provided below.

_____   _____

                                              _____

                                              _____

                                              _____

                                              _____

                                              _____

_____

_____

_____

_____

_____

_____

_____

_____

_____

_____

_____

_____

_____

_____

_____

_____

_____

_____

_____

_____

- Enc. Information pack
- Dear Mr Gardiner
- 10 Mansfield Industrial Park
- 18 January 201_
- Thank you for your above-mentioned enquiry. We are pleased to send you enclosed our complete information pack on our Intelligent Energy Saving Lamps for home lighting. For information on our complete range of products please see our website.
- Attention: Mr Edward Gardiner
- HN / cf
- Yours sincerely
- Paul Seubert
- Tel.: +49 721 450520

- UK
- 76228 Karlsruhe
- Export Manager
- The Handyman DIY Market
- **Lumen Energiesparlampen GmbH**
- Salisbury
- SP9 4RG
- An den Feldern 13–17
- Fax: +49 721 4505211
- *Paul Seubert*
- E-Mail: info@lumen-sparlampen.com
- www.lumen-sparlampen.com
- Lumen Energiesparlampen GmbH
- Your enquiry of 15 January 201_

Grammar refresher

Language and grammar: Currencies and singular / plural nouns

Währungsbezeichnungen

Abkürzungen für Währungen stehen **vor** der Ziffer mit Zwischenraum und werden groß geschrieben.

| EUR 200 | USD 2,750,500 | GBP 35,000 |

Symbole für Währungen stehen **vor** der Ziffer ohne Zwischenraum.

| €200 | $2,750,500 | £35,000 |

Ausgeschriebene Bezeichnungen für Währungen stehen hinter der Zahlenangabe (in der Regel im Plural) und werden klein geschrieben.

| eight euros | fifty dollars | five pounds Sterling |

Wörter, die im Englischen entweder nur im Singular oder nur im Plural vorkommen

Nur Singular		Nur Plural	
Ausgabe(n)	expenditure	Dank	thanks
Information(en)	information	Geschäftsräume,	premises
Ausrüstung(sgegen-	equipment	Firmengrundstück	
stände)		Kleidung	clothes
Erzeugnis(se)	produce	Meerenge	straits
Fortschritt(e)	progress	Umgebung	surroundings
Geschäft(e)	business	Verdienst	earnings
Hausaufgabe(n)	homework	Ware(n)	goods
Kenntnis(se)	knowledge		
Leute	people		
Möbel(stücke)	furniture		
Nahrung(smittel)	food		
Rat, Ratschläge	advice		
Unannehmlichkeiten	inconvenience		
Ware(n)	merchandise		

peoples – Völker

Please translate the following sentences into English.

1. Unsere Ausgaben beliefen sich auf 7365,50 Euro.

   _____

2. Die Nachrichten aus seinem Heimatland waren sehr deprimierend.

   _____

3. Wir bedauern die Unannehmlichkeiten, die durch dieses Versehen entstanden sind.

   _____

4. Wir suchen einen Exportleiter mit guten Französischkenntnissen.

   _____

5. Diese Informationen über seine Geschäfte sind vertraulich.

   _____

Phrases refresher

1 **Put in the correct prepositions from the box to complete the phrases.**

by • for (4x) • of (2x) • on • to (4x)

1. Thank you _____ your letter _____ 23 May.

2. We refer _____ our discussion _____ 18 June.

3. We would now like to ask you _____ a detailed offer _____ stainless steel bins.

4. I'm afraid, we cannot agree _____ this proposal.

5. I'm sorry, this is quite unacceptable _____ us.

6. We would like to apologize _____ this delay.

7. We need a reply _____ Friday at the latest.

8. We hope this proposal will be _____ interest _____ you.

2 **Ending the correspondence on a friendly note is important. Complete the following phrases.**

1. We look forward to _____ again.

2. We hope to _____ soon.

3. We look forward to a long and fruitful _____.

4. We look forward to welcoming _____.

5. We hope this proposal _____ to you.

6. We hope this information _____.

7. Thank you for _____.

8. Should you have any further questions, please _____.

stainless steel – Edelstahl

Unit refresher

1 Restore the correct order of these jumbled elements of an enquiry by drawing lines between the numbers (1.–7.) and the appropriate letters (a.–g.).

1.

a. **Subject: Small vertical axis wind turbines for domestic and commercial use**

2.

b. We are a major German company active in the field of renewable energy. We specialise in the installation of small commercial and domestic units. As you will be aware there is considerable interest in environmentally-friendly sources of energy and a rapidly expanding market for these products here in Germany.

3.

c. Yours sincerely
Dietmar Schmeding
Moderne Energietechnik GmbH

4.

d. We would be grateful if you could send us sales literature and full specifications. We would also be pleased if you could arrange a demonstration for one of our experienced engineers.

5.

e. Dear Sirs

6.

f. Assuming the demonstration is positive we would place a trial order. We would then expect to place regular orders in future.

7.

g. We saw an article in the March issue of the journal *Renewable World*, which gave a positive assessment of your innovative products.

2 Sie arbeiten im Einkauf der deutschen Sportbedarfskette SportPlatz AG. Auf der Website des schottischen Herstellers Scots Outdoors haben Sie eine interessante Allwetterjacke entdeckt. Schreiben Sie eine E-Mail unter Berücksichtigung folgender Punkte:

– Kurze Vorstellung Ihrer Firma mit Hinweis auf Firmenprofil im Anhang
– Verweis auf Website von Scots Outdoors
– Bitte um Details zu Allwetterjacken (*hard shell jackets*), aus neuartigem Material
– Anfrage zu Liefer- und Zahlungsbedingungen für Aufträge über 3000 Stück pro Artikel
– Schlusssatz

From: einkauf@SportPlatz.com
To: info@scotsoutdoors.co.uk
Sent:
Subject:

Attachment: Company profile

vertical axis – senkrechte Achse

3

◎ A 3.9

Francesca Schmitt, who works for a small upmarket chain selling designer furniture is anxious to find a supplier for furniture by a particular designer. She decides to ring a British company she has found on the internet. Listen to the dialogue and decide whether the following statements are TRUE or FALSE.

	TRUE	FALSE
1. Francesca is trying to find a supplier for furniture designed by Bob Jackson.	☐	☐
2. Damien Chandler's German is nearly fluent.	☐	☐
3. Francesca's company is a retailer of designer furniture.	☐	☐
4. Damien says she should buy the furniture from an agent in Germany.	☐	☐
5. She would require 6 sets of garden furniture and 30 stackable chairs.	☐	☐
6. Damien Chandler offers to send her a quote.	☐	☐
7. He says she will hear from him very soon.	☐	☐

4

Refer to the information on discounts in your student's book and complete the anagram. Put in the missing parts of the expressions describing the different kinds of discounts.

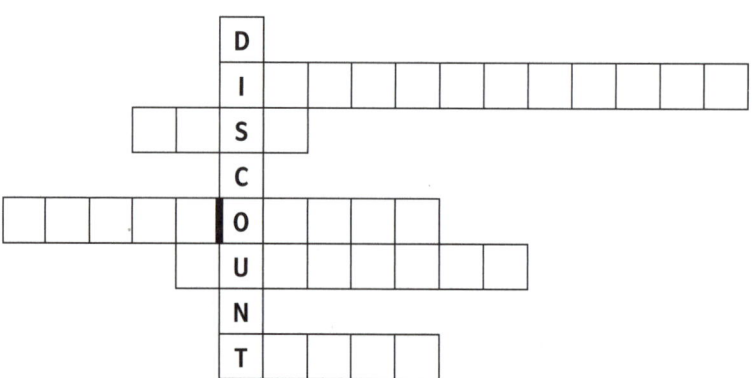

Grammar refresher

Language and grammar: Adjectives

Little / few, much / many
Little (= wenig) und *much* (= viel) werden für **nicht Zählbares** verwendet.
She has **little** knowledge of bookkeeping.   There was not **much** time left.
Few (= wenige) und *many* (= viele) werden für **Zählbares** verwendet.
Few people left before the end of the show.
Are **many** of our clients affected by the storm?

Tipp: *Much / many* werden vorzugsweise in **Verneinungen und Fragen** verwendet.
In **bejahten** Sätzen werden sie durch *a lot of, lots of, a great deal of, plenty of, a (large) number of* ersetzt.
There isn't much information on their website.
How many people attended the meeting?
There is a lot of information on their website.
A large number of people attended the meeting.

!

Steigerung dieser Adjektive
little – less – least   **few – fewer –fewest**
The **less** trouble there is, the **fewer** worries you have.
much – more – most   **many – more - most**
Last month we heard **more** about it and **most** of the information was true.

stackable – stapelbar

1 Complete the sentences using the correct translation for the words in brackets.
Try to use different words for *viel* as appropriate.

1. It is said that the company has received _____ (**viele**) complaints.

2. He has been doing _____ (**viel**) travelling lately.

3. _____ (**Wenige**) people learn Latin nowadays.

4. I'm awfully sorry – I haven't _____ (**viel**) time at the moment.

5. The house is quite large – we have _____ (**viel**) space to put up guests.

6. He is said to have _____ (**viel**) money.

7. You haven't told me anything new. I had already received _____
(**den größten Teil**) of the information.

8. He had had _____ (**wenig**) opportunity to acquire qualifications.

9. Do you expect to meet _____ (**viel**) opposition to your plans?

10. There was _____ (**weniger**) interest in the product than we had hoped.

Language and grammar: Adverbs

Adverbien ohne -*ly*
He walks very **fast**. They worked **hard** on the project (hardly = kaum).
He turned round (roundly = rundheraus).
She arrived **late** for the meeting (lately = kürzlich).
We flew **direct** to India (directly = sofort).

Bildung von Adverbien von Adjektiven, die auf -*ly* enden
Adjektive, die auf -*ly* enden, wie *friendly, timely* bilden das Adverb durch
Umschreibung.
He welcomed us **in a friendly manner.**
They completed the task **in time.**

Englische Verben statt deutsche Adverbien
I **happened** to meet him in London (= zufällig).
I **hope** to see you there (= hoffentlich).
He **is likely** to be in the office (= wahrscheinlich).
Prices **are expected** to rise (= voraussichtlich).
They **are said** to be in serious trouble (= angeblich).
I **prefer** working in a large office (= lieber).
It **seemed** that nobody knew anything about it (= anscheinend).
She **was about** to leave for the airport (= gerade) when Helen rang.
After a short break he **continued** to search the internet for information (= weiter).
He **likes** to work out in a gym before work (= gerne).

---

2 Translate the sentences in the last paragraph of the Language and grammar
box above into German. Use German adverbs instead of the English verbs.

Example: I happened to meet him in London. = Ich habe ihn zufällig in London getroffen.

Phrases refresher

1 Study the phrases in your student's book and fill in the missing words from memory.

1. We have visited your _____ and are interested in …

2. We have obtained your _____ from the chamber of commerce.

3. Your services have been recommended to us by a _____.

4. We saw your _____ for biros in the May issue of *Stationery World*.

5. We are a leading importer with excellent _____ all over the UK.

6. We are a well-established _____ of tools.

7. We are a young and rapidly growing firm _____ in the production of …

2 A polite tone is essential for successful business communication in English. Choose a suitable expression from the box to formulate a polite request. In some cases there are several possible solutions.

> Please • Could you please • We would be grateful • Can you • Could you • May we ask you • We would welcome • Would you be so kind • We would appreciate • would be appreciated

1. _____ possibly state your earliest delivery date?

2. _____ send us a cost estimate for the repair of the doors?

3. _____ for a detailed quotation.

4. _____ let us have a brochure and a price list.

5. _____ it if you could quote your most favourable prices.

6. _____ as to arrange for someone to pick me up at the station?

7. _____ grant us an introductory discount on this article?

8. _____ if you attached your export price list.

9. _____ guarantee delivery by the end of the month?

10. _____ to send us samples of the leather used?

11. _____ if you sent us more information on article RH700.

12. _____ enclose 1000 leaflets for distribution at the fair.

13. Any additional information you can give us _____ .

14. _____ a presentation of the new system in our office.

15. _____ for information on your terms of payment.

16. _____ it if you could mail us a brochure.

17. _____ to inform us more in detail about the smartphone?

18. _____ it if you would inform us without delay.

19. Delivery within three weeks _____ .

20. _____ as to book a conference room for the meeting?

Unit 10   Offers

Unit refresher

1 The number and size of orders received will largely depend on the offers made to win them. Decide whether the following statements are TRUE or FALSE. Refer to your student's book.

	TRUE	FALSE
1. You should reply to enquiries promptly.	☐	☐
2. Do not personalise salutations as it may sound impolite.	☐	☐
3. Come straight to the point in the first sentence without referring to the enquiry to save the reader's time.	☐	☐
4. If you cannot make an offer right away, let the prospective customer know that his/her enquiry will be processed as soon as possible.	☐	☐
5. Keep your offer as concise as possible and do not provide information that has not been asked for.	☐	☐
6. Don't praise your own firm. That would make a bad impression.	☐	☐

2 ⊚ A 3.10 Thomas Dahlke has just arrived in Dorchester on the south coast of England to do a course in business English and improve his general English skills. Listen to him talking to Rupert Hannington, the director of studies.

1. What level is Thomas' English?

   _____

2. What is Mrs Broadbent's cottage like?

   _____

3. What subject does she know a lot about?

   _____

4. When does Thomas have his business English lessons?

   _____

5. What does the school offer on Wednesday afternoons?

   _____

6. Whose job is it to sort out any problems students may have?

   _____

7. Does the school offer courses on Saturday and Sunday?

   _____

8. Is there much night life in Dorchester?

   _____

9. How is Thomas afraid he may be spending his evenings?

   _____

3 You work for the German company Energietec GmbH. You take a phone call from Andrew Murchison at Modern Heating Systems plc in Manchester in which he says that their engineer (George Osborne) would like to call at your factory on 22 or 23 March or one week later on 29 or 30 March, whichever is more convenient. They are especially interested in your company's vertically mounted double helix wind turbines. There is a morning flight that would get Mr Osborne to Munich airport at about 11.30, return flight at 16.30. Would one afternoon be enough or would it be better to stay until the following day? If so, could we recommend a medium quality hotel in the vicinity. He needs instructions on the best way to get from the airport to your company.

Write a memo in German to Xaver Lipke, the export manager.

Energietec GmbH		**Telefonnotiz**
Für: _____		Datum: _____
Von: _____		

4 Sie arbeiten bei der Firma SchneiderFilter GmbH (E-Mail: verkauf@schneiderfilter.com). Ihre Firma vertreibt in Europa die Produkte des kanadischen Herstellers AFC Filters. Sie haben von Caroline Bates von der britischen Firma Bates & Goddard (E-Mail: bates@bates-goddard.co.uk) eine Anfrage für das Modell HE304 erhalten.

Schreiben Sie Ms Bates eine E-Mail und berücksichtigen Sie dabei folgende Punkte:

- CC: tomlinson@afc-filters.com
- Dank für Anfrage
- Normalerweise gesamtes Sortiment von AFC-Wasserfiltern vorrätig
- Modell HE304 wegen eines unerwarteten Großauftrags leider z. Zt. nicht auf Lager
- Anfrage sofort an den Hersteller, AFC Filters in Vancouver, weitergeleitet; AFC Filters wird sich direkt mit Ms Bates in Verbindung setzen
- Entschuldigung wegen Unannehmlichkeiten und Hoffnung auf erneute Kontakte bei späterem Bedarf

Grammar refresher

Language and grammar: this / these, that / those; each / every; which / what

This (Sing.) und *these* (Plur.) beziehen sich auf das räumlich oder zeitlich **Nähere**.
That (Sing.) und *those* (Plur.) beziehen sich auf das räumlich oder zeitlich **Entferntere**.
If I were you, I'd take **this** shirt here; **that** shirt in the window isn't big enough for you.
All **these** cars (here) will be sold within a month, but **those** cars (over there) won't be easy to sell.
We have been informed **this** morning. I clearly remember **that** year when we had snow in May.
These last few hours have been decisive for the project. We have achieved more than in all **those** months before.
This weist auf etwas **Folgendes** hin.
That bezieht sich auf etwas, das **bereits erwähnt** wurde oder bekannt ist.
The system works like **this**: ... I have told you **that** many times.

---

vertically mounted double helix wind turbines – Doppelhelix-Windturbinen mit senkrechter Achse

Each wird für **eine oder mehrere Personen / Sachen aus einer kleinen Anzahl** verwendet. Die Betonung liegt sehr deutlich auf der einzelnen Person / Sache.
Every wird für **mehrere Personen / Sachen aus einer größeren Anzahl** verwendet. Die Betonung liegt stärker auf der gesamten Gruppe.
Last week we got three offers. **Each** is interesting for a different reason.
You will find our products in **every** part of the world. **Every** airport in Europe was affected by the strike.

Which wird bei Fragen verwendet, wenn aus einer **bestimmten, begrenzten Anzahl** ausgewählt wird.
What wird bei Fragen verwendet, wenn aus einer **unbestimmten, großen Menge** ausgewählt wird.
Which model would you prefer? The green one or the grey one? **Which** of the three positions advertised is he applying for?
What is your favourite colour? **What** can I do for you? **What** job would you like?

1 Delete the incorrect pronoun in the following sentences.

1. They've got three different diaries. **What / Which** do you prefer?
2. The three winners of the competition were announced. **Each / Every** winner received a prize.
3. **What / Which** profession do you think he will eventually take up?
4. I like **these / those** T-shirts here. I'm not so wild about **these / those** over there.
5. We drive to the coast **each / every** weekend.
6. What about **this / that** book here? It looks more interesting than **this / that** one.
7. We will acknowledge **every / each** donation.

2 Please translate these sentences into English.

1. Bitte füllen Sie diese Formulare sorgfältig aus.

   _____

2. Ich fahre jeden Tag mit dem Rad ins Büro.

   _____

3. Was möchten Sie zum Essen *(with your meal)* trinken?

   _____

4. Welchen Saft soll ich *(would you like me to)* für Sie bestellen, Orangensaft oder Apfelsaft?

   _____

5. Ab Januar wird jeder Auftrag angenommen und innerhalb eines Monats bearbeitet *(to process)*.

   _____

6. Ich habe diese Zeitung ausgelesen. Bring mir bitte die Zeitungen dort.

   _____

7. Ich habe ihm das schon dreimal erklärt, aber er hat es immer noch nicht begriffen.

   _____

8. Leider können wir nicht jede Anfrage sofort beantworten, da wir so viele erhalten haben.

   _____

   _____

Phrases refresher

1 Put in the missing words. The solutions are given in scrambled form in brackets after the blanks.

1. Many thanks for your _____ [qeuiyrn] of 30 November.

2. Should you have any _____ [hrutefr] queries, please contact us.

3. I hope this quotation will find your _____ [aporpval].

4. We are pleased to _____ [uoqet] as follows: …

5. Delivery can be made ex _____ [stcko].

6. We can offer 15 % discount on _____ [sroedr] for at least 100 units.

7. We grant 2 % cash _____ [tuocdsni] for payment within 10 days.

8. We take pleasure in submitting the following _____ [tcso] estimate.

9. This offer is without _____ [anggetneme].

10. Our _____ [uulas] terms of payment are: 30 days net, 10 days 2 %.

11. Payment is to be made by irrevocable and confirmed _____ [letret] of credit.

12. We are sending you enclosed our latest _____ [cueagalot].

13. We would request payment by bank _____ [trnrsfea].

14. We are pleased to hear that you are _____ [estiderent] in our copiers.

15. Our terms of _____ [vidylere] are: EXW Leipzig.

16. Prices are _____ [stcjebu] to change without notice.

17. The offer is subject to _____ [iorpr] sale.

18. We look forward to _____ [emgicnlwo] you as our customers.

19. Regular _____ [mtoerscsu] are granted open account terms.

2 Choose the correct prepositions from the box.

about • at (2x) • for • in • of • on (2x) • to (2x) • until • with (3x)

1. We take pleasure _____ submitting the following quotation: …

2. We offer you firm 5,000 cordless hedge trimmers _____ a unit price of €28.50.

3. Our terms of payment are either cash _____ order or cash _____ delivery.

4. Please transfer the invoice amount _____ our account _____ Derbyshire Bank.

5. Many thanks for your enquiry _____ 29 December _____ shelving units.

6. We would like to draw your attention _____ our special offer for garden furniture.

7. Your order will be dealt _____ promptly and carefully.

8. Our staff will be pleased to assist you _____ any time.

9. This offer is firm _____ 31 July.

10. We offer 10 % quantity discount _____ orders _____ 1000 units or more.

Unit 11 Orders

Unit refresher

1 You work for Dream Interiors Ltd, 30 Stockport Lane, Altrincham, Cheshire WA6 7AX,
e-mail: dreaminteriors@mail.com. Your boss asks you to order the following by e-mail
from Romantica Cottons, attention Sue Goring (Mrs), e-mail: romantica@mail.com:

- 30 duvet covers 140 x 190 cm in Rose Pink stripe with matching pillowcases 80 x 80 cm
- 20 duvet covers in Boy Blue stripe 140 x 190 cm with matching pillowcases 80 x 80 cm
- When will delivery be effected?
- Prices as per trade price list; remind them about agreed introductory 5 % discount
- Payment: by cheque on delivery

2 Listen to the following telephone conversation between David Freeman, who has a
design boutique for furnishings in Leeds, Yorkshire, with International Design Ltd, a
distributor of furniture design labels.

◎ A 3.11

1. What precisely does the customer wish to order?

   _____

2. How long will it take to process the order?

   _____

3. What communication will the customer receive from the haulier?

   _____

4. How does the customer wish to pay?

   _____

5. Which department deals with payments?

   _____

6. How will confirmation of the order and payment be sent?

   _____

3 Sie arbeiten im Einkauf der Sportbedarfskette SportPlatz AG, E-Mail:
einkauf@SportPlatz.com. Sie haben ein günstiges Angebot für Allwetterjacken
von dem schottischen Hersteller Scots Outdoors erhalten. Erteilen Sie einen
Auftrag per E-Mail und berücksichtigen Sie dabei Folgendes:

- Datum: 15. März dieses Jahres, Auftragsnummer: AW/GB/03/11
- Ansprechpartner: Donald Stuart, E-Mail: donald.stuart@scotsoutdoors.co.uk
- Dank für gestriges Angebot
- Bestellung von Allwetterjacken (*hard shell jackets*) in 3 Herren- und 4 Damengrößen,
  siehe beigefügtes Auftragsformular
- Auftrag wird auf der Basis der angehängten Allgemeinen Geschäftsbedingungen
  (in Englisch) erteilt
- Versprochene Lieferzeit von 3 Wochen Voraussetzung für den Auftrag
- Bitte um Benachrichtigung bei Übergabe der Sendung an Spediteur
- Bitte Lieferanschrift beachten

duvet cover – Bettbezug; haulier – Spediteur

4 **Insert these jumbled elements into the purchase order form below.**

Mr Donald Stuart • CIP Heusenstamm, Germany • 230 York Road • UK • £109.50 •
SportPlatz AG Zentrallager • North Berwick • 30 days net, 10 days 2% • Germany •
EH3 5PW • Otto-Hahn-Str. 85 • 100 each • S, M, L, XL • 63151 Heusenstamm •
Women's Hard Shell Jacket Ben Macdui • 100 each • £109.50 • +49 6106 361-29 •
£43,800 • L, XL, XXL • within 3 weeks • (signature) • £32,850 • AW/GB/03/11 •
15 March 201_ • Thomas Koehler • Scots Outdoors • Men's Hard Shell Jacket Ben Nevis •

SportPlatz AG

Sportbedarf
Taunusallee 58, 60486 Frankfurt
Tel. +49 69 345621-0, Fax +49 69 34561-11, www.SportPlatz.com

Purchase Order

Order Number: _____   **Date:** _____
Must appear on all related correspondence,
shipping documents and invoice

To: **Deliver to:**

_____   _____

_____   _____

_____   _____

_____   _____

_____   **Tel.:** _____

_____   **Contact:** _____

Please supply:

Quantity	Description	Sizes	Unit Price	Total Price
_____	_____	_____	_____	_____
_____	_____	_____	_____	_____

Terms of delivery: _____

Terms of payment: _____

Delivery: _____

Authorized by: _____
                  (your own name)
                  for SportPlatz AG

Grammar refresher

Language and grammar: Relative pronouns

a) Bei Menschen: who, who(m), that, whose
Nominativ: The person **who** rang was simply asking for information.
Akkusativ: The woman **whom** they have appointed CEO comes from a well-known multinational. The woman **that** they have appointed CEO comes from a well-known multinational.
Bei diesem Beispiel wäre auch Folgendes möglich: The woman **(...)** they have appointed CEO comes from a well-known multinational. (Im Akkusativ kann das Relativpronomen weggelassen werden.)
In der gesprochenen Sprache ginge auch: The woman **who** they have appointed CEO comes from a major multinational.
Genitiv: The finance director, **whose** photo appeared in yesterday's papers, is expected to resign.

b) Bei Gegenständen und Tieren: which, that, of which
Nominativ: The furniture, **which** is well-designed, will complement our range.
Akkusativ: The goods **that** you ordered will be shipped tomorrow.
Dieser Satz könnte ebenfalls lauten: The goods **(...)** you ordered will be shipped tomorrow. (Das Relativpronomen *that* kann weggelassen werden, s.o.)
The goods **which** you ordered will be shipped tomorrow. (Im Akkusativ ist sowohl *that* als auch *which* möglich.)
Genitiv: *Whose* wird seltener bei Gegenständen verwendet; stattdessen benutzt man *of which*.
The company, the directors **of which** have been accused of mismanagement, is expected to file for insolvency. (Wortstellung beachten!)

Achtung: Vor *that* oder **(...)** (= weggelassenem Relativpronomen) steht nie ein Komma.

!

Delete as appropriate; (...) means the relative pronoun can be left out.

1. The horse **who/which** was injured in the accident was taken to the vet.
2. The man **which/whom** they have appointed director of human resources is a trained psychologist.
3. The man **(...)/which** you were talking to is my immediate superior.
4. The apprentice, **who/whose** exam results were excellent, was offered a job in the export sales department.
5. They export their instruments, **which/who** have a good reputation, all over the world.
6. Our products, **the special features of which/which special features** are described in the enclosed brochure, can be delivered from stock.
7. The company, **whose/which** products have received several awards, is seeking to expand.
8. The woman **that/which** I was talking to is a buyer from Germany.

Phrases refresher

1 The second half of every second word has been deleted. Complete these words with the help of the list below.

Thank y_____ for yo_____ e-mail.

W_____ have stu_____ your quot_____ and wo_____ now li_____ to or_____

2 un_____ each o_____ the mod_____ ABC a_____ CDF a_____ the pri_____ stated

i_____ your lat_____ price li_____. Your pri_____ are quo_____ CIF Ham_____ and

pay_____ will b_____ made b_____ irrevocable a_____ confirmed let_____ of cre_____.

Please ackno_____ this or_____ promptly.

W____ look for_____ to hea_____ from y_____ in t_____ very ne_____ future.

[acknowledge]	[letter]	[quoted]
[and]	[like]	[studied]
[and]	[list]	[the]
[at]	[models]	[units]
[be]	[near]	[We]
[by]	[of]	[We]
[credit]	[order]	[would]
[forward]	[order]	[you]
[Hamburg]	[payment]	[you]
[hearing]	[prices]	[your]
[in]	[prices]	
[latest]	[quotation]	

2 Delete the incorrect alternatives.

1. Please supply the following items **on / at** the terms stated below.
2. We **would like / like** to order article 7455.
3. Please **notice / note** that delivery within two weeks is essential.
4. We look forward to **do / doing** further business with you.
5. The goods must reach us **until / by** 30 May at the latest.
6. Please **make sure / care for it** that the china is packed with utmost care.
7. As agreed payment will be **affected / effected** by bank transfer.
8. The prices are taken **from / out of** your price list of 1 October.
9. We are pleased to **attach / add** our Purchase Order no. 7015.
10. Please **let the goods be transported / arrange for transport of the goods** by air freight.
11. The import licence is valid **until / by** 31 July.

Unit refresher

1 Fill in the crossword. You will find the words you need in your student's book.

Across

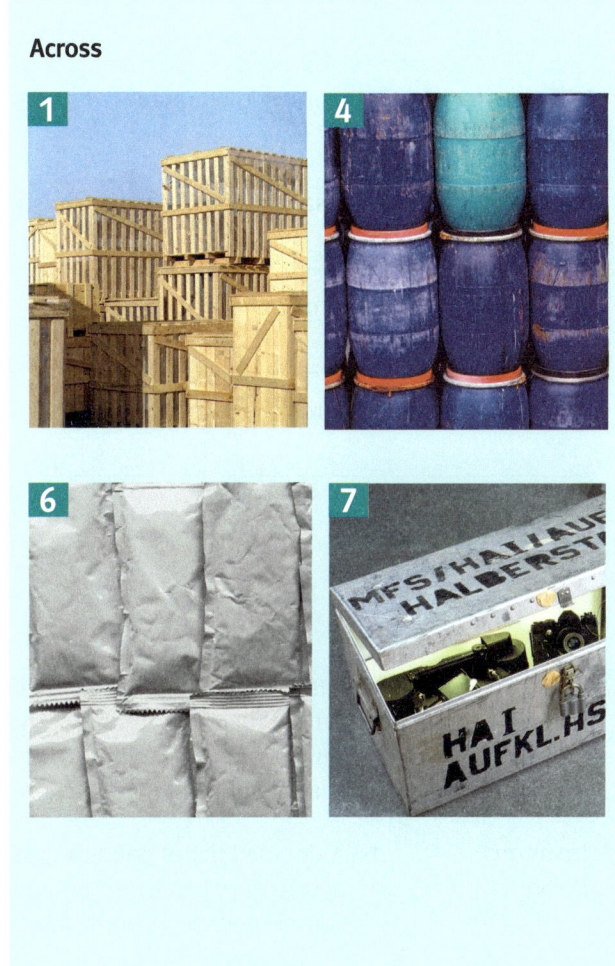

Down

2 Listen to this discussion on the radio between a freight forwarder
◎ A3.12 and an environmentalist. Then answer the questions.

1. What causes a lot of the congestion on major EU routes?

   _____

2. For what part of a journey are trucks indispensable?

   _____

3. Why has freight transport by road increased so dramatically?

   _____

4. What are the biggest disadvantages of road transport?

   _____

5. Give two disadvantages of rail transport?

   _____

6. What other alternative to road transport is mentioned?

   _____

3 Match the documents (1.–7.) with the appropriate explanations (a.-g.) and draw lines.
Use a dictionary, if necessary.

1. Proforma Invoice	a. A formal document stating the name of the country from which the goods mainly originate. It is required by the authorities in the importing country for customs, import quota and statistical purposes.
2. Insurance Policy	b. A detailed list of goods supplied, showing transport details and requiring the buyer to pay the total amount stated therein within the period agreed upon.
3. Packing List	c. A freight document used in multimodal and sea transport which must not be dirty. It is unique among transport documents in being a documentary proof of ownership.
4. Certificate of Origin	d. A document that is both a receipt for goods and a record of the existence of a contract of carriage by road, rail or air.
5. Bill of Lading	e. A sample invoice giving a potential buyer information about prices and conditions of sale, enabling a potential importer to apply for an import licence.
6. Commercial Invoice	f. A list of the contents of a particular case or container, enabling the recipient to check the contents on arrival.
7. Waybill/ Consignment Note	g. A contract by which one party, in return for a payment called a premium, binds himself to pay the person named in the contract a certain sum of money when a stated event happens.

4 Sie arbeiten in der Exportabteilung der Firma Lumen Energiesparlampen GmbH, An den Feldern 13–17, 76228 Karlsruhe, exports@sparlampen.com und bearbeiten den Auftrag eines Kunden aus Zypern, der eine Lieferung Energiesparlampen dringend für die Ausstattung eines neuen 5-Sterne-Hotels benötigt, dessen Eröffnung kurz bevorsteht.

Richten Sie eine E-Mail-Anfrage an die Transportagentur Top Freight Management, contact@top-freight.com, und berücksichtigen Sie dabei Folgendes:

- Bitte um kurzfristiges Angebot für Transport per Luftfracht Karlsruhe – Limassol, Zypern
- 600 Stück Energiesparlampen in zwei Kartons, Abmessungen: 600 x 400 x 400 mm, Bruttogewicht je 12,4 kg
- Abholort: Karlsruhe, Ankunftsflughafen: Larnaka, Zypern, Bestimmungsort: Limassol, Zypern
- Abholung: morgen bis 16:00 ab Werk Karlsruhe
- Ankunft beim Empfänger bis spätestens 3 Arbeitstage ab Abholung
- Empfängeranschrift: Michelis Andreou Ltd, Haidariou Street 25, Limassol, Cyprus
- Empfänger könnte Ware gegebenenfalls selbst am Flughafen Larnaka abholen

Grammar refresher

Language and grammar: Word order

Im Gegensatz zur flexiblen deutschen Satzstellung, bei der das Objekt an den Satzanfang treten kann, wird im Englischen im Allgemeinen die Reihefolge Subjekt – Prädikat – Objekt eingehalten. Soll das Objekt zur Hervorhebung am Satzanfang stehen, muss es zum Subjekt eines Passivsatzes gemacht werden. **!**

Subject	**Predicate**	**Object**
His secretary	arranges	all his appointments.
All his appointments	are arranged	by his secretary.

Position of adverbials

Satzbezogene adverbielle Bestimmungen, z.B. *almost, also, carefully, certainly, ever, gladly, naturally, nearly, never, obviously, often, only, really, rightly, still, successfully,* etc., dürfen – anders als im Deutschen – **nicht** zwischen Prädikat und Objekt gesetzt werden! Sie stehen in der Regel:
- vor dem Verb, wenn das Prädikat kein Hilfsverb aufweist: In the past they **often** complained about the regulations.
- hinter dem (ersten) Hilfsverb: The trainees have **also** been working hard on this project until now.
- hinter einer Form von *to be*: It was **certainly** a most successful fair.

Adverbielle Bestimmungen der Zeit, z.B. *last week, next year, in 2010,* etc., und des Ortes, z.B. *here, at the airport, in Britain,* etc., stehen gewöhnlich am Satzanfang oder am Satzende: **In the last few years** prices have remained stable **in the UK**.

Achtung: Am Satzende ist eine vom Deutschen abweichende Reihenfolge zu beachten. **Ort vor Zeit**: I met him **at the fair last June**. = Ich habe ihn im vergangenen Juni auf der Messe getroffen. **!**

1 **Mark the spot [*] where the adverbial (in brackets) could be inserted. In some cases there are several options.**

1. (mainly) They deal in textiles manufactured in India.
2. (rightly) Her work was praised by the experts on the panel.
3. (often) He helped to solve similar problems when we were travelling through the desert.
4. (for generations) The company has been famous for this article.
5. (also) I am very upset. My briefcase has been stolen.
6. (this afternoon, from the airport) I am going to pick them up.
7. (never) Our prices have been undercut by the competition.

2 **Please translate the sentences.**

1. Der Bericht wird bestimmt nächste Woche fertiggestellt.

   _____

2. Meine Chefin sieht immer zuerst ihre E-Mails durch, bevor sie mit der Arbeit beginnt.

   _____

3. Auch die Qualität der Messer ist nicht mehr so gut wie früher.

   _____

4. Wir werden die Waren Anfang nächster Woche nach Australien verschiffen.

   _____

5. Der Exportleiter hat das Formular genau geprüft, bevor es weitergeleitet wurde.

   _____

Phrases refresher

Put in the correct form of the verbs in brackets. In some cases several solutions are possible.

1. We are pleased to inform you that the desks can now _____ (abholen) at our works.
2. The container _____ (übergeben) to the freight forwarders today.
3. Yesterday the consignment _____ (verladen) on board MS Dorothea.
4. Next week the plants _____ (verschicken) by air freight to Athens.
5. Normally, our smoke detectors _____ (verpacken) in sturdy cardboard boxes.
6. Please _____ (liefern) the equipment on one-way pallets.
7. We trust that the spare parts _____ (ankommen) in time before the fair.
8. We feel sure that the reliability of our sensors _____ (entsprechen) your expectations.
9. At the moment the garments _____ (transportieren) by lorry to Milan.
10. We hope that your customers _____ (gefallen) with our designer belts.

Unit refresher

1 Sie arbeiten bei Lumen Energiesparlampen GmbH und bearbeiten den Auftrag eines Kunden aus Zypern. Füllen Sie das untenstehende Rechnungsformular aus und berücksichtigen Sie dabei Folgendes:

- Datum: 17. Januar dieses Jahres
- Empfänger: Michelis Andreou Ltd, Haidariou Street 25, Limassol, Zypern
- Kundennummer: CY/144/2
- Rechnungsnummer: 3204/CY
- Bezeichnung der bestellten Energiesparlampen: Classic Star, 11 W, E 14
- Stückpreis 11,50 Euro, abzüglich 10 % Mengenrabatt
- Anzahl: 600 Stück
- Lieferbedingungen: CIP Limassol, Zypern
- Zahlungsbedingungen: 30 Tage nach Rechnungsdatum

Lumen Energiesparlampen GmbH

An den Feldern 13–17
76228 Karlsruhe
Tel.: +49 721 450520
Fax: +49 721 4505211
E-mail: info@lumen-sparlampen.com
www.lumen-sparlampen.com
USt. ID No. DE 712 034 988

To: _____

_____

_____

_____

Customer No. _____

Date: _____

Contact: (your name)

_____

Tel.: +49 4505225

Invoice No. _____

Quantity	Description	Unit Price Euro	Total Price Euro
_____	Energy saving lamp _____ less _____ Terms of delivery: _____	_____ Total:	6,900.00 _____ _____

Please remit the invoice amount to our account with Badenbank eG, BIC: BDBADEKA;

IBAN: DE 49 66090801 0087654321 within _____.

2 Listen to the dialogue on preferred means of payment, then decide whether the following statements are TRUE or FALSE.

A 3.13

	TRUE	FALSE
1. The interviewee generally pays cash at the supermarket.	☐	☐
2. He uses his debit card to buy newspapers and the odd sandwich.	☐	☐
3. He rarely uses his credit card.	☐	☐
4. Banks want to phase out cheques as they are expensive to process.	☐	☐
5. The interviewee has an electrical engineering business.	☐	☐
6. He pays his taxes online.	☐	☐

3 Sie arbeiten im Rechnungswesen der Sportbedarfskette SportPlatz AG. Ihr Chef hat nachstehende Zahlungserinnerung eines schottischen Lieferanten erhalten. Herr Renner sagt zu Ihnen: „Antworten Sie David Fraser, bitten Sie um Entschuldigung und erklären Sie die Verzögerung. Sie wissen ja, was bei uns los war. Versprechen Sie ihm, dass wir die Überweisung noch heute veranlassen werden."

Beantworten Sie per E-Mail die Zahlungserinnerung für Herrn Renner.

From:	david.fraser@scotsoutdoors.co.uk		
To:	jakob.renner@SportPlatz.com	Cc:	donald.stuart@scotsoutdoors.co.uk
Sent:	14 May 201_	Attachment:	Invoice No. G / 4431

Subject: Invoice No. G / 4431, Your Order No. AW / GB / 03 / 11

Dear Mr Renner

According to our records the above invoice in the amount of £76,650, dated 7 April 201_, has not been settled. The invoice, a copy of which is attached, was due on 8 May.

We look forward to your early settlement of this outstanding account.

Yours sincerely
David Fraser
Accounts

4 Please translate using a dictionary, if necessary.

The problem with reminders is that the supplier both wants to obtain his/her money and maintain the customer's goodwill. Reminders should, therefore, be persuasive, tactful and, like all other business communications, customer-oriented. In many cases a telephone call produces better results than an e-mail, fax or letter. Sometimes several reminders have to be sent to achieve the desired result with the tone of the correspondence becoming more and more insistent.

Grammar refresher

Language and grammar: Modale Hilfsverben – wollen und dürfen

Wollen kann man keinesfalls immer mit *want* übersetzen; es hat im Englischen eine Reihe von unterschiedlichen Entsprechungen:
Want (man verwendet es nur, wenn es sich um einen Wunsch handelt)
Was für eine Stelle willst du haben? = What kind of job do you want?
Plan / intend (diese Verben entsprechen „wollen", wenn es sich um eine Absicht oder einen Plan handelt)
Die Regierung will die Mehrwertsteuer erhöhen. = The government plans / intends to raise VAT.
Going to (ist ebenfalls eine Entsprechung für „wollen", wenn es sich um eine Absicht handelt)
Wie wollen Sie auf den Brief reagieren? = How are you going to react to the letter?
Hinweis: *was just going to / about to* entsprechen dem Ausdruck „wollte gerade"
Ich wollte Sie gerade auf Ihrem Handy anrufen. = I was about to / just going to ring your mobile.

Dürfen hat ebenfalls mehrere Entsprechungen im Englischen:
May (höfliche Bitte)
Dürfen wir uns Ihnen anschließen? / Dürfen wir uns dazu setzen? = May we join you?
Be allowed to (ausdrückliche Erlaubnis / ausdrückliches Verbot)
Sie dürfen an öffentlichen Orten nicht rauchen. = Your are not allowed to smoke in public places.
Probably (Vermutung)
Sie dürften mit den Verkaufszahlen zufrieden sein. = They are probably satisfied with the sales figures.

Please translate the following sentences.

1. Was wollen Sie mit den Artikeln machen, die nicht verkauft worden sind?

    _____

2. Wann will der Chef den Bericht haben?

    _____

3. Seine Vorgesetzte dürfte mit seiner Arbeit unzufrieden sein.

    _____

4. Man darf ohne Fahrkarte nicht in den Zug einsteigen.

    _____

5. Die Regierung will den Konsum ankurbeln *(boost)*.

    _____

6. Darf ich Ihnen etwas anbieten?

    _____

7. Ich wollte gerade das Büro verlassen, als ein wichtiger Kunde anrief.

    _____

Phrases refresher

1 **Put in the correct words from the box.**

> account • amount • balance • collection • deadline • explanation • extension • instalments • matter •
> option • payment • settlement • statement • steps

1. The invoice _____ is now four weeks overdue.

2. You have not given us any _____ for the delay in payment.

3. The _____ of account shows a _____ of £7,250
   in our favour.

4. We should be grateful for an early _____ of our invoice.

5. We must insist that you make _____ by 31 July at the latest.

6. Should you fail to meet this _____ we shall have no _____
   but to take legal _____.

7. Unless you remit the amount in time, we will hand the _____ over to a
   _____ agency.

8. We have instructed our bank to transfer the sum to your _____ with ABO Bank.

9. We are afraid we must ask you for an _____ of four weeks.

10. We suggest that we pay in three _____ of €10,000 each.

2 **Study the phrases in your student's book and answer the following questions.**

1. What options does a supplier have when he has sent at least two reminders to a customer who has failed to meet the deadline set in the reminders?

   _____

   _____

   _____

   _____

2. What may be offered as plausible reasons for a delay in payment?

   _____

   _____

   _____

3. What options could a debtor request if he is unable to pay the full invoice amount in time?

   _____

   _____

Unit refresher

1 Insert words from the box to complete the following e-mail.

completion • estimate • inspected • paint • premises • quality • reception • repainting • satisfied • urgently

From: peterbainbridge@office.com
To: j.mcneil@mail.com
Sent: 201_-03-09
Subject: Re-decoration of business **1** _____ at 124 Shoreham Road

---

Dear Jonathan

I recently **2** _____ the progress of work at the above offices.

I am afraid that I am not at all **3** _____ with the standard of work.

Doors and woodwork show traces of the old **4** _____ and in places

the new gloss paint has run. The paint needs removing and the doors

5 _____. The walls are still uneven although you quoted £1,800 in

your **6** _____ to rectify this. Finally, the paint on the walls of the

7 _____ area is neither the shade nor **8** _____

stipulated.

I should be grateful if you would deal with this situation immediately. I should point out that

we need the offices **9** _____ and it will obviously now take longer

than planned. Your estimate gave 10 working days for the **10** _____

of the work, which we confirmed. Please let me know asap when the work can be completed

to the required standard.

Yours

Peter Bainbridge
Fosters Ltd

2

A 3.14

Listen to this conversation between a business woman and a waiter. Decide whether the following statements are TRUE or FALSE.

	TRUE	FALSE
1. The woman has ordered beef Stroganoff.	☐	☐
2. She will have to wait about 40 minutes for her food.	☐	☐
3. There is not enough staff in the kitchen.	☐	☐
4. The customer would like to cancel her order.	☐	☐
5. She refuses a glass of wine.	☐	☐
6. She decides to do some work on her laptop.	☐	☐
7. The restaurant does not accept credit cards.	☐	☐

3 Sie arbeiten im Einkauf der Sportbedarfskette SportPlatz AG, E-Mail: einkauf@ SportPlatz.com. Sie hatten bei Scots Outdoors, E-Mail: donald.stuart@scotsoutdoors. co.uk, je 100 Allwetterjacken für Damen und Herren bestellt, die fristgerecht geliefert wurden. Inzwischen haben Sie von Ihren Kunden einige Reklamationen erhalten.

Senden Sie Scots Outdoors eine Mängelrüge und berücksichtigen Sie dabei Folgendes:

- Datum: 8. August 201_, Auftragsnr. AW/GB/03/11, Ansprechpartner: Donald Stuart
- Fast alle Jacken inzwischen verkauft
- Im Vormonat 10 Reklamationen wegen Allwetterjacken für Damen *(women's hard shell jackets)*: Kunden brachten Jacken zurück, Nähte kräuselten sich *(seams got crinkly)* nach dem Waschen
- Empfohlene Waschtemperatur von 40 Grad soll eingehalten worden sein, Nähgarn *(sewing thread)* offenbar für die empfohlene Waschtemperatur nicht geeignet
- Alle 10 Jacken wurden von SportPlatz zurückgenommen und Kaufpreis ersetzt
- Rücksendung einer Jacke an Scots Outdoors als Beweis
- Erklärung von Scots Outdoors erbeten
- Weitere Aufträge abhängig von der Erledigung dieser Reklamation

4 **You are Fiona Campbell and work with Scots Outdoors as Donald Stuart's assistant. The German sports gear chain SportPlatz AG has returned one women's hard shell jacket Ben Macdui the seams of which are crinkly. SportPlatz claims that they had to take back 10 jackets because this defect had appeared after washing. Adjust this complaint:**

- Date: 15 August 201_
- Defective jacket has now been examined: sewing thread used for one batch indeed of inferior quality
- Only one batch (10 units) affected, all other jackets sewn with suitable thread
- Scots Outdoors prepared to compensate SportPlatz in full for the loss
- The equivalent of GBP 1,095.00 will be transferred to the account of SportPlatz
- Apologies for inconvenience caused
- Pleased to hear that jackets are selling well
- Closing sentence: hope for further orders

Grammar refresher

Language and grammar: If or when?

Das deutsche **wenn** wird im Englischen mit *if* wiedergegeben, wenn zuerst eine **Bedingung** erfüllt werden muss, bevor etwas geschieht oder eintritt. In diesen Fällen muss man die Konjunktion **wenn** im deutschen Satz durch **falls** ersetzen können.
I'll see you in August if I have time. (Es ist nicht sicher, dass ich Zeit haben werde.)
Ich sehe dich im August, wenn (falls) ich Zeit habe.

Das deutsche **wenn** wird im Englischen mit *when* wiedergegeben, wenn es sich um ein **zeitliches Ereignis** handelt. In diesen Fällen muss man im Deutschen **wenn** durch **dann**, **wenn** ersetzen können.
I'll see you in August when I come back. (Es ist sicher, dass ich zurückkomme.)
Ich werde dich im August sehen, (dann) wenn ich zurückkomme.

Bei allgemeinen Aussagen über Tatsachen, die immer so sind, kann sowohl *if* als auch *when* verwendet werden.
If / When you heat metal, it expands. Wenn (Falls / Dann, wenn) man Metall erhitzt, dehnt es sich aus.

1 **If or when? Delete as appropriate.**

1. We'll have the office party outside **if**/**when** it doesn't rain this evening.
2. **If**/**When** trading starts in New York tomorrow, share prices are sure to react negatively to the bad news.
3. **If**/**When** I received the complaint, I immediately began to investigate the matter.
4. She will be 21 **if**/**when** she completes her training course.
5. We will have to pay a hefty fine **if**/**when** we do not install new emission filters.
6. **If**/**When** the fire alarm went off, we all rushed to the car park.
7. **If**/**When** it makes you happy, I'll buy you a new computer.
8. **If**/**When** I knew that they are honest, I would lend them the money.
9. **If**/**When** the secretary had finished the report, she went home.
10. **If**/**When** they heard the results, they were overjoyed.

2 **Complete the sentences using your imagination.**

1. We would be glad if _____.
2. When the telephone rang _____.
3. I would apply for the job if _____.
4. We will let you have the information when _____.
5. If we had been granted the credit _____.
6. You would be taking a great risk if _____.
7. We would have consulted a lawyer _____.
8. When I wake up tomorrow _____.

Phrases refresher

1 **Choose the correct prepositions from the box.**

> at • by • for (2x) • in (2x) • of (2x) • on (2x) • out • to (4x) • up • with

1. We are writing _____ reference _____ our order no. AB/151.

2. _____ unpacking the cases we found that 10 cups were missing.

3. We are sorry to point _____ that the quality is not up to standard.

4. The damage must have happened _____ transit.

5. Our order must have been mixed _____ with another customer's order.

6. Please arrange _____ the immediate dispatch of the goods.

7. We would ask you to cut the price _____ the original sum of £3,250.

8. We would suggest that you grant us a price reduction _____ 10 %.

9. Thank you _____ drawing this problem _____ our attention.

10. We will inform you _____ the steps taken in due course.

11. We are pleased to say that the replacements are now _____ their way to you.

12. Please return the defective items _____ our expense.

13. We are prepared to reduce the price _____ 15 %.

14. The order was carried out _____ accordance with the contract.

15. The matter will be settled _____ your satisfaction.

2 **Complete the sentences by translating the adjectives / adverbs in brackets.**

1. We regret to inform you that the pillow cases are

   _____ (verschmutzt).

2. The damage must be due to _____ (unsachgemäß) handling.

3. We would ask you to replace the _____ (mangelhaft) Waren.

4. Please have the _____ (schadhaft) mixers collected at our warehouse.

5. We will examine the matter _____ (gründlich) and inform you at once.

6. We are afraid that several units are _____ (schwer) damaged.

7. The tables are _____ _____ (stark zerkratzt).

8. We are keeping the _____ (zerbrochen) plates at your disposal.

9. Please send us the _____ (fehlend) articles without delay.

10. We trust that you will settle the matter _____ (rasch) and to our entire satisfaction.

Unit 15 Marketing products and services

Unit refresher

1 You work for Mobilia Ltd, e-mail: a.eastman@mobilia.co.uk. Your boss (Alexander Eastman) tells you to send an e-mail to Felicity Metcalf at VenturePR, e-mail: metcalf@venturepr.com, covering the following points:

- 50th anniversary of Mobilia Ltd next June
- Plan to celebrate with major event: afternoon and evening gig, theme: 1960s songs; weekend garden party for about 200 invited guests – suggest and organise venues/catering
- Merchandising: e.g. quality pens engraved with company logo/designer key rings/other suggestions?
- Press coverage: TV/internet/newspapers/design magazines; PR emphasis on state-of-the-art technology and design, not on tradition
- Suggest appointment for week after next – any time Tuesday or Wednesday to discuss rough draft and cost estimate

2 ⊚ A 3.15 Listen to Jamie and Arthur, two 23-year-olds, who have rented a small shop, talking to Amanda, a marketing friend. They plan to open a furnishing and accessories boutique with a difference called Young Abode. Answer the following questions.

1. What colours have Jamie and Arthur chosen for the shop interior and façade?

   _____

   _____

2. What age group do they plan to appeal to?

   _____

3. What kind of people do they expect to buy their products?

   _____

   _____

4. Have they done any kind of research before setting up their shop?

   _____

   _____

5. What does Amanda mean when she says they have to "position their company clearly"?

   _____

   _____

6. How does Amanda suggest they should make their brand distinctive?

   _____

   _____

3 Ihr Unternehmen hat seine Geschäftstätigkeit in Großbritannien ausgeweitet und die Geschäftsleitung überlegt, dort ein kleines Büro zu eröffnen. Ihre Chefin ist sich jedoch über die Vorgehensweise noch nicht ganz im Klaren. Sie hat nebenstehende Anzeige gefunden und bittet Sie, den Text für sie sinngemäß ins Deutsche zu übertragen.

Progressys plc
The serviced office people

Need an office to work from?

Avoid all the hassle of renting, furnishing and equipping an office plus the pitfalls and problems involved in employing secretarial staff.

Move into your new fully equipped office tomorrow – with or without secretarial services – in a prestigious building.

✓ Any size from 10 m²
✓ Short-term, flexible or long-term leases
✓ Tailored to your needs and budget
✓ Available in top locations in all major cities throughout the UK
✓ Limits costs with predictable overheads
✓ Flexible to grow, downsize or relocate as your needs dictate
✓ Modern purpose-built premises
✓ Ideal for start-ups just getting off the ground
✓ Special terms for small companies

We also have virtual offices to suit all budgets:
✓ Top address worldwide
✓ Dedicated mailbox with forwarding
✓ Personalized call answering service
✓ Full business support services

Conference rooms, business lounges or rooms to meet clients available at short notice.

Call us on +448 846 376 1990 to discuss your requirements or download full details on www.progressys.com.

4 Study the texts on e-commerce in your student's book and decide whether the following statements are TRUE or FALSE.

	TRUE	FALSE
1. Traditional retailing is growing faster than online retailing.	☐	☐
2. All supermarkets offer online ordering facilities to their customers.	☐	☐
3. The wholesaler's B2B services enable retailers to do their ordering at night.	☐	☐
4. Online reviews written by other consumers make prices less transparent.	☐	☐
5. Sponsored links on search sites are an effective marketing tool.	☐	☐

lease – Mietvertrag; overheads – Fixkosten; start-up – junges Unternehmen; purpose-built premises – für diesen Zweck gebaute Geschäftsräume; business lounge – Empfangshalle

Grammar refresher

Language and grammar: Indirect (reported) speech

Eine Aussage kann entweder wortwörtlich zwischen Anführungsstrichen zitiert oder als Bericht wiedergegeben werden.

Direkte Rede: "I am planning to attend the meeting", the boss said.

Indirekte Rede: The boss said he was planning to attend the meeting

1. Wenn in der indirekten Rede das Verb im einleitenden Satz im Präsens steht, ändert sich nichts.

   Direkte Rede: "I work for the local authority."

   Indirekte Rede: He **says** he **works** for the local authority.

2. Wenn das Verb im einleitenden Satz im *Simple past* steht, verschiebt sich das Tempus wie folgt:

   Direkte Rede: "I work for the local authority."

   Indirekte Rede: He **said** he **worked** for the local authority.

Present tense wird zu *Simple past*, *have* wird zu *had* und *will* wird zu *would*.

"I am applying for a new job." – She **said** she **was** applying for a new job.

"We have finished the work." – They **told** him (that) they **had** finished the work.

"We will pick you up at 2 am." – Julia **said** (that) they **would** pick her up at 2 am.

Hinweis: *Would* und *could* bleiben unverändert:

I would be pleased to assist. – She assured us (that) she would be pleased to assist. Wird eine wörtliche Aussage später berichtet, können logische Änderungen erforderlich sein, z. B. kann aus „*I*" „*he*" oder „*she*", aus „*here*" „*there*", aus „*this*" „*that*" oder aus „*last year*" „*the year before*" werden.

Im Deutschen kann der Konjunktiv verwendet werden, um die indirekte Rede zu markieren: Er **sagte**, er **könne / könnte** an dem Meeting nicht teilnehmen.

Dies hat im Englischen keine Entsprechung; stattdessen ist das Tempus gegenüber der direkten Aussage verschoben, wenn das einleitende Verb im *Simple past* steht. Der Satz lautet daher: He said he **could** not attend the meeting.

1 Put the following sentences into indirect speech.

1. She says, "I am very pleased about the way my job is developing."

   _____

2. He told them, "I will arrive in the morning and hope to be at your office by 12 am."

   _____

3. They informed him, "We have finished the report and can let you have it by Friday."

   _____

4. He assured them, "I would appreciate it if you would take a more active part in planning."

   _____

5. "I'm afraid I can't attend the AGM this year", he wrote.

   _____

6. The sales manager said: "I expect prices to rise in the near future."

   _____

2 Please translate these sentences into English.

1. Er sagt sein Bruder sei in den Vereinigten Staaten.

_____

2. Der Lieferant versprach, die Teile würden am Montag geliefert.

_____

3. Der Chef teilte ihr mit, dass er das Flugzeug in New York versäumt habe.

_____

4. Sie erwiderte, dass sie die Besprechung in London absagen werde.

_____

5. Die Sekretärin betonte, dass sie die E-Mail nicht erhalten habe.

_____

Phrases refresher

Match the excerpts from advertisements (1.–9.) with the products (A–I) by drawing arrows.

1. a must-have gizmo for the amateur chef

2. combines perfect chic and amazing capacity

3. ideal for sensitive skins

4. it has an easy to use touchscreen

5. latest technology of truly diminutive dimensions

6. state-of-the-art design and technology

7. the ultimate in hand-crafted silver jewellery

8. tried and tested Swiss craftsmanship

9. you will be bewitched by the dazzling design

A

B

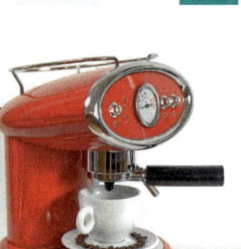

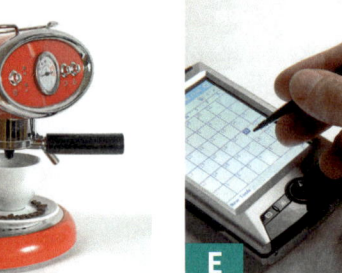

C   D   E

F   G

H   I

Unit refresher

1 Fill in the crossword puzzle on the EU.

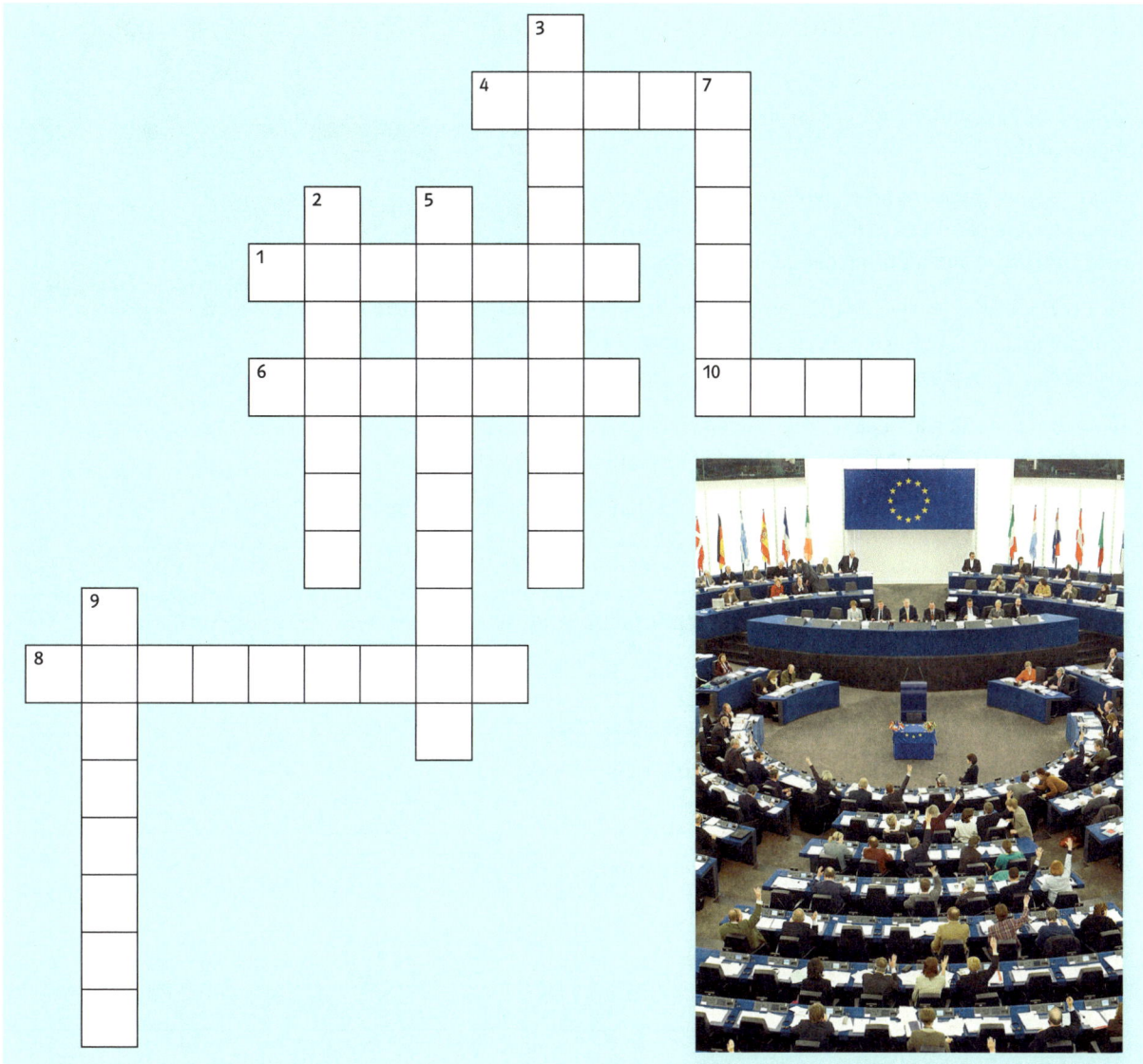

Across

1. Bulgaria and … joined the EU in 2007.
4. One of the EU's central principles is the free movement of …
6. The most widely spoken foreign language in the EU.
8. He or she is appointed by the member states for 2 years.
10. Common currency adopted by many member states.

Down

2. Political decisions are taken by the … of Ministers.
3. EU institution that introduces regulations.
5. EU institution whose members are elected in the member states.
7. The EU is a … market.
9. Seat of the European Commission.

2 You see the advertisement below in a magazine and as you will be free in the summer months you decide to apply. Follow the instructions in the advertisement.

Sussex Polyglot Ltd | Brighton – Bournemouth – Eastbourne
Tel.: +44 1276 287 148 | E-mail: sussexpolyglot@co.uk

VACANCIES FOR SOCIAL LEADERS

Why not work as a social leader with one of our language schools on the South Coast of England in June, July, August 201_?

Practise your English, gain experience of working with young people of all nationalities and earn a small salary with free board and accommodation into the bargain.

As a social leader you will help to organise programmes of sports and games, cultural outings and evening activities for foreign students aged 14+.

If you are over 18 and already have a good command of English write a brief e-mail giving reasons why you would be good at this job. Send it off today with your CV as an attachment.

You will receive full information and details of salary and working hours by e-mail.

3 Listen to the job interview with Sascha Schmidt from Schwerin and answer the questions.

A 3.16   1. Why does Sascha want to change jobs?

_____

2. Who would he have to interact with in his new job?

_____

3. What do his references show according to Jonathan Pope?

_____

4. How does Sascha rate his Spanish?

_____

5. What does Sascha mention as his weakness?

_____

6. How much does he know about the company he is applying for a job with? Where did he get the information?

_____

7. Why is he confident he would enjoy living in Britain?

_____

8 Why can't they give him a decision straight away?

_____

9. Is Sascha heading straight back for Germany?

_____

Grammar refresher

Language and grammar: Comma and hyphen

Komma

Es gibt im Englischen keine gleichmäßig angewandten Regeln wie im Deutschen. Man setzt ein Komma, wenn es für das Verständnis des Satzes erforderlich ist.

Ein Komma **kann** man setzen

- wenn der Nebensatz vor dem Hauptsatz steht: If the boots had been cheaper, we would have bought them right away.
- vor und / oder nach Wörtern wie *however, unfortunately, moreover, of course, in addition, furthermore, though, thus, too,* etc.: Our service team will, of course, be pleased to assist you at any time.

Ein Komma **muss / sollte** man setzen

- bei Aufzählungen: The United Kingdom consists of England, Scotland, Wales, and Northern Ireland.
- vor und nach Einschüben in den Satz: Many service industries, notably catering, are dominated by small firms.
- vor und nach für das Satzgefüge entbehrlichen Relativsätzen, die nur zusätzliche Information liefern: We trust that our latest catalogue, which we are sending you as an attachment, will give you all the details.

Achtung: Im Gegensatz zum Deutschen steht im Englischen kein Komma **vor** einem Nebensatz: We are sure that your customers will be prepared to pay a little more for our stylish belts.

!

Bindestrich

Ob ein Bindestrich gesetzt, auseinander oder zusammen geschrieben wird, bleibt weitgehend dem Schreiber überlassen. Man findet gleichermaßen *flower-pot, flower pot* und *flowerpot.*

Ein Bindestrich wird häufig gesetzt

- in zusammengesetzten Adjektiven, wenn der zweite Teil auf *-ed* oder *-ing* endet: short-lived, state-owned, well-known, the decision-making process.
- wenn eine Vorsilbe vor ein großgeschriebenes Wort tritt: ex-President, un-American, pro-British.

Achtung: Im Zweifelsfalle empfiehlt es sich die Wörter ohne Bindestrich und auseinander zu schreiben. Der Bindestrich ist im Englischen bei weitem nicht so oft erforderlich wie im Deutschen und zusammengesetzte Wörter sind im Englischen eher selten.

!

Put in commas where possible.

1. I am sure that they will make us a favourable offer.
2. Unfortunately we are not able to supply these articles at the present time.
3. The new director of finance who has worked for a well-known multinational is only 29 years old.
4. They said they would cancel the order if deadlines were not observed.
5. When you order online you should make a note of the reference number.
6. In addition we offer a 10 % end of season discount.
7. If you order immediately we can deliver within 24 hours.
8. Many companies especially small and medium-sized firms find it difficult to obtain credit at present.
9. Of course we always try to cater for companies' special requirements.
10. The person that they have appointed is a business school graduate.

Phrases refresher

1 Match the German terms for schools and examinations (1.–13.) with the appropriate translations or paraphrases in English (a.–m.) by drawing lines.

1.	Allgemeine Hoch-schulreife (Abitur)	a.	certificate enabling a student to continue education at higher vocational school
2.	Berufskolleg	b.	business college
3.	Berufschule	c.	chamber of commerce examination
4.	Fachhochschule	d.	commercial school
5.	Fachhochschulreife	e.	comprehensive (school)
6.	Fachoberschulreife	f.	German higher education entrance qualification
7.	Gesamtschule	g.	German university entrance qualification
8.	Gymnasium	h.	grammar school
9.	Hauptschule	i.	higher secondary school
10.	IHK-Prüfung	j.	secondary modern school
11.	Höhere Handels-schule	k.	state examination in English for clerical and administrative professions
12.	KMK-Zertifikat	l.	university of applied science/polytechnic university
13.	Realschule	m.	vocational school

2 Complete the sentences by choosing the right expressions from the box.

> application • at short notice • business college • main subjects • names of referees • on a placement • on the off-chance • opportunity to use • position advertised on • skills • some experience in • traineeship at

1. I should like to apply for the _____ your website.

2. I have just completed my _____ Schwarzweiß & Co. KG.

3. I would welcome the _____ my Spanish.

4. I have _____ the wholesale trade.

5. From March until July I attended a _____ in Berlin.

6. I would be able to start _____.

7. I have good translating and proof-reading _____.

8. I should be happy to provide the _____.

9. I am applying _____ that you may have a vacancy.

10. I spent four weeks in Edinburgh _____.

11. My _____ included social studies and geography.

12. I hope that you will consider my _____ suitable.

Prüfungsvorbereitung KMK-Fremdsprachenzertifikat

Struktur der Prüfung

In der schriftlichen Prüfung zum KMK-Fremdsprachenzertifikat sollen Sie zeigen, dass Sie
- gesprochene und geschriebene Informationen in Englisch verstehen können (Kompetenzbereich Rezeption).
- Schriftstücke aus dem Berufsleben selbstständig schreiben können (Kompetenzbereich Produktion).
- Texte oder gesprochene Mitteilungen von der einen in die jeweils andere Sprache übertragen können (Kompetenzbereich Mediation).

Sie erhalten für den schriftlichen Teil maximal 100 Punkte.

Die mündliche Prüfung bietet Ihnen Gelegenheit, Ihre mündliche Kommunikationsfähigkeit zu zeigen, indem Sie alleine sprechen, mit anderen oder ganz allgemein Gespräche führen oder auch dolmetschen (Kompetenzbereich Interaktion). Sie erhalten für den mündlichen Teil maximal 30 Punkte.

Zum Bestehen der Prüfung ist jeweils mindestens die Hälfte der möglichen Punkte im schriftlichen und mündlichen Teil notwendig.

Schriftliche Prüfung

Die Dauer der schriftlichen Prüfung richtet sich nach der Niveaustufe.

KMK Stufe I	60 Minuten
KMK Stufe II	90 Minuten
KMK Stufe III	120 Minuten

(Vereinzelt werden auch Prüfungen auf Stufe IV angeboten, 150 Minuten.)

Kompetenzbereich Rezeption

Hier geht es um Ihre Fähigkeit, gesprochene und geschriebene Mitteilungen verstehen zu können. Erster Teilbereich ist eine Hörverstehensaufgabe. Sie sollen hierbei aus dem gesprochenen Text Informationen auf Deutsch wiedergeben. Zweiter Teilbereich ist eine Leseverstehensaufgabe. Zu einem vorgegebenen Text bearbeiten Sie Fragen in offener Form oder Auswahlform.

Kompetenzbereich Produktion

In diesem Kompetenzbereich sollen Sie zeigen, wie gut Sie englische Dokumente erstellen können. Typische Prüfungsinhalte sind das Verfassen einer Kurzmitteilung (z. B. E-Mail, Fax) oder eines Geschäftsbriefes. Möglich ist z. B. auch die Gestaltung einer Kundeninfo, eines Flyers oder einer Handlungsanweisung in Englisch.

Kompetenzbereich Mediation

Es geht hier um Ihre Fähigkeit, zwischen Kommunikationspartnern zu vermitteln und Informationen von der einen in die jeweils andere Sprache übertragen zu können. Dieser Prüfungsteil enthält sowohl rezeptive als auch produktive Elemente, d. h. Sie müssen Informationen aufnehmen und auswerten und diese dann weitergeben können. Mögliche Handlungssituationen sind hier z. B. die inhaltliche Wiedergabe einer englischsprachigen Werbebroschüre, einer E-Mail oder einer Gesprächsnotiz.

Im Folgenden finden Sie Übungsaufgaben und Bearbeitungshinweise für die Vorbereitung auf die schriftliche Prüfung (Seiten 74–130), im Anschluss folgen Hinweise und Tipps für die mündliche Prüfung (Seiten 131/132) sowie ein Musterbeispiel für ein KMK-Fremdsprachenzertifikat (Seiten 133/134).

Bearbeitungshinweise

Bei diesen Musteraufgaben haben Sie die Möglichkeit herauszufinden, welche Prüfungsteile Ihnen besonders liegen und in welchen Prüfungsteilen Übungsbedarf besteht. Die einzelnen Prüfungstypen sind hier exemplarisch in verkürzter Form dargestellt.

Die Lösungsvorschläge finden Sie auf der beigefügten CD-ROM zum Workbook.

AUFGABE 1   ◎ A3.17

Rezeption: Hörverstehen

Sie arbeiten bei der Firma Design Unlimited GmbH in Würzburg. Ihre Firma nahm letztes Jahr bereits mit Erfolg an der Neuheitenmesse British Newcomer Show in London teil. Sie sollen die wichtigsten Daten für die Anmeldung zur diesjährigen Messe herausfinden. Sie rufen deshalb die Info-Hotline an und hören den Ansagetext zur British Newcomer Show. Hören Sie sich die Ansage zweimal an. Beantworten Sie die folgenden Fragen auf Deutsch.

Nr.	Frage	Antwort
1.	Wann findet die Ausstellung statt?	
2.	Die Ausstellung öffnet jeweils um	
3.	Die Ausstellung schließt täglich um	
4.	Wo findet die Ausstellung statt?	
5.	Besteht eine Parkmöglichkeit, wenn ja, für wie viele Fahrzeuge?	
6.	Wie viele Aussteller werden erwartet?	
7.	Was wird ausgestellt?	
8.	Wie viel kostet eine Eintrittskarte für die Preisverleihung?	
9.	Wann sind Mitarbeiter telefonisch erreichbar?	
10.	Unter welcher Telefonnummer kann man Karten bestellen?	

AUFGABE 2

Sie arbeiten in einem Internethandelsunternehmen. Ihre Firma überlegt, die Produktpalette zu erweitern. Sie werden deshalb beauftragt den folgenden Artikel in deutscher Sprache auszuwerten. Beantworten Sie folgende Fragen auf Deutsch.

Amazon puts corn flakes on menu

Amazon is now offering 2,000 basic packaged foods as part of its drive to become the number one destination for online consumers. Shoppers can pick up 70 individual Kellogg's Corn Flakes portions for $28. If more than $25 is spent, Amazon also pays for delivery – a decision experts say that shows its determination to take on other discount and mail order grocers. The focus on bulk sales of non-perishable items allows the firm to take on big US names like Wal-Mart and Costco.

While founder Jeff Bezos had aimed to turn Amazon into the Wal-Mart of electronic retailing when he launched the group 10 years ago, with a company mantra of "get big fast", the company recently revealed a drop in net profit for the last three months. Despite a small rise in sales, net profit for the three months to 31 December came in at $199m (£112m), compared to $347m the year before. Analysts have suggested that Amazon may be losing market share to traditional retailers such as Wal-Mart and Target, as well as auction sites like eBay and even search internet site Google.

But the company is not just targeting the "pile 'em high, sell 'em cheap" end of the market. Under its "gourmet food" section, shoppers can buy filet mignon steaks, food gift baskets and even French truffles. And the more discerning shopper in search of a bargain can save more than $3,500 on a 4lb tin of Russian Beluga caviar in Amazon's sale – paying $9,120 for a tin. But whether the strategy will pay off has yet to be seen.

Quelle: BBC NEWS

1. Welches Ziel verfolgt Amazon?

   _____

2. Ab welchem Einkaufswert wird versandkostenfrei geliefert?

   _____

3. Was kann der Kunde für 28 USD auswählen?

   _____

4. Auf welche beiden Firmen zielt die Strategie von Amazon ab?

   _____

5. Welches Firmenmotto verfolgte Jeff Bezos bei der Gründung von Amazon?

   _____

6. Wie hat sich der Gewinn nach Steuern in den letzten drei Monaten des Vorjahres verändert?

   _____

7. Wie schätzen Analysten die Entwicklung des Marktanteils von Amazon ein?

   _____

8. Welche Angebote in Amazons Produktpalette zeigen, dass die Firma nicht ausschließlich die Verkaufsstrategie „viel und billig" verfolgt?

   _____

AUFGABE 3

Produktion

Sie arbeiten bei der Firma GlobalSoft Inc. Da Ihr Unternehmen auf dem amerikanischen Markt expandieren möchte, wird die Firma an einer Messe in Chicago teilnehmen. Um die Sales Promotion mit Werbegeschenken zu unterstützen, haben Sie den Auftrag bei Werbeartikelherstellern in den USA weitere Informationen einzuholen. Ihr Ausbilder bittet Sie, eine E-Mail an die Firma Giveaways Unlimited mit folgendem Inhalt zu schreiben:

- Sie sind im Internet auf die Firma und ihre Produkte aufmerksam geworden.
- Bitten Sie um Zusendung folgender Materialien:
  – Gesamtkatalog und spezieller Winterkatalog
  – Muster aus dem Go Green-Sortiment für umweltfreundliche Produkte
- Fragen Sie, welche Extrakosten für Verpackung und Versand für den 24-Stunden Express Service innerhalb der USA anfallen.
- Erkundigen Sie sich, ab welcher Bestellmenge Preisnachlässe gewährt werden.
- Formulieren Sie einen höflichen Schlusssatz.

From:	uk@globalsoft.com
To:	info@giveaways-unlimited.com
Sent:	(today's date)
Subject:	Enquiry

AUFGABE 4

Mediation

Ihr Chef möchte für das englische Tochterunternehmen ein Onlinebanking-Konto eröffnen und gibt Ihnen einen Flyer der Riversdale Bank Ltd. Er bittet Sie den entsprechenden Abschnitt sinngemäß auf Deutsch wiederzugeben. Ihr Unternehmen macht im Augenblick einen Jahresumsatz zwischen 7 und 8 Millionen Euro.

Online services for business customers

1. **Turnover less than 1m Euros**
   Business Online Banking
   ✓ Manage your day-to-day banking from your PC round the clock: check accounts, apply for a loan or overdraft, pay bills and suppliers, move money.

2. **Turnover 1m to 10m Euros**
   Business Master Online
   ✓ Manage your day-to-day banking from your PC round the clock: check accounts, apply for a loan or overdraft, pay bills and suppliers, move money. Also book business events, access the latest information relevant to your sector and share our panel's expert opinions.

3. **Turnover above 10m Euros**
   Internet Treasurer Platinum
   ✓ A suite of applications designed for large corporates, offering real-time access to information and portability. The system can be used internationally.

Bearbeitungshinweise

- Lesen Sie vor dem ersten Hören des Textes die Aufgaben durch. Dadurch erhalten Sie eine Vorstellung des Textinhaltes.
- Prüfen Sie bei Zahlen und Größenangaben in der Aufgabenstellung immer, ob die Angabe im Deutschen identisch ist. Zum Beispiel das englische *billion* bedeutet im Deutschen „Milliarde" und nicht „Billion".
- Stimmen die Namen, die genannt werden mit denen in der Aufgabenstellung überein? Hier ist Vorsicht geboten, denn so werden vermeintlich richtige Aussagen falsch.
- Achten Sie beim Hören wichtiger Schlagwörter darauf, ob es sich um eine positive oder eine negative Aussage handelt.
- Die komplette Aussage der Frage sollte im Hörverstehenstext enthalten sein. Werden in der Frage weitere Informationen aufgeführt, die im Dialog gar nicht angesprochen werden, so ist die Aussage falsch.
- Auf *false friends* achten! Diese Wörter könnten absichtlich falsch ins Deutsche übersetzt worden sein. Zum Beispiel heißt *actually* „eigentlich" und nicht „aktuell". Insbesondere beim Hören können *false friends* leicht Verwirrung stiften.

AUFGABE 1   ◎ A3.18

Sie hören zehn Namen. Tragen Sie die Namen in die entsprechenden Kästchen ein.

Nr.	Name
1.	
2.	
3.	
4.	
5.	
6.	
7.	
8.	
9.	
10.	

AUFGABE 2   ◎ A3.19

Sie hören Ihren Anrufbeantworter ab, auf dem eine Nachricht hinterlassen wurde. Hören Sie aufmerksam zu und tragen Sie die Angaben in die entsprechenden Kästchen ein. Hören Sie sich die Nachricht zweimal an.

Name	
Order no.	
Phone no.	

AUFGABE 3

A3.20

Sie hören Ihren Anrufbeantworter ab, auf dem eine Nachricht hinterlassen wurde. Hören Sie aufmerksam zu und tragen Sie die Angaben in die entsprechenden Kästchen ein. Hören Sie sich die Nachricht zweimal an.

Name																				
Order no.																				
Phone no.																				

AUFGABE 4

A3.21

Sie hören Ihren Anrufbeantworter ab, auf dem eine Nachricht hinterlassen wurde. Hören Sie aufmerksam zu und tragen Sie die Angaben in die entsprechenden Kästchen ein. Hören Sie sich die Nachricht zweimal an.

Name																				
Order no.																				
Phone no.																				

AUFGABE 5

A3.22

Sie machen gerade ein Praktikum in der englischen Niederlassung Ihres Unternehmens. Sie sind diese Woche in der Personalabteilung und nehmen an einem Einstellungsgespräch teil. Die Leiterin der Human Resources Abteilung bittet Sie, während des Gesprächs mit dem neuen Kollegen den Bewerberbogen mit den notwendigen Informationen zu ergänzen.

APPLICATION FOR EMPLOYMENT

Name: _Benning James Peter_   Date: _____

Street: _15 Liverpool Street_

City: _Manchester MN5 3XY_

Telephone: _____

1. Position applied for: _PA in the dispatch department_____
2. How did you hear of this job? _____
3. When can you start? _____
4. Are you looking for full time employment?   ☐ Yes   ☐ No
5. Are you willing to work shift?   ☐ Yes   ☐ No
6. Are you willing to work weekends?   ☐ Yes   ☐ No
7. Any other skills, qualifications or experience we should consider:

   _____

8. Employment history (most recent employer):
   Company name: _SalesTalk_   City: _Dover_____
   Date started: _____   Date ended: _____
   Responsibilities: _____

   _____

   Reason for leaving: _____
   Name of superior: _____   May we contact? ☐ Yes ☐ No

AUFGABE 6

@ A3.23

Sie hören ein Interview, das in der Radiosendung Business Talk gesendet wird. Hören Sie aufmerksam zu und beantworten Sie die folgenden Fragen auf Deutsch. Hören Sie sich den Text zweimal an.

Nr.	Frage	Antwort
1.	Welche Position hat Mr Dixon bei Dixon Corporation?	
2.	Welche zwei Vorteile von Videokonferenzen nennt Mr Dixon?	
3.	In welchen Bereichen wurden die Reisekosten reduziert?	
4.	Wie versucht man technischen Problemen vorzubeugen?	
5.	Was passiert, wenn es wirklich einmal zu einem Netzwerkausfall kommt?	
6.	Welchen Nachteil hat die Teilnahme an einer Videokonferenz für Teilnehmer, z.B. aus Japan?	
7.	Welche Probleme werden genannt, die Geschäftsreisende bei Reisen in ferne Länder haben?	
8.	Welche Vorteile von Videokonferenzen nennt Mr Dixon in Bezug auf seine Mitarbeiter?	
9.	Was ist ein wichtiger Bestandteil der Unternehmensphilosophie der Dixon Corporation?	
10.	Wie versucht Dixon Corporation diesen Teil der Unternehmensphilosophie außerdem umzusetzen?	
11.	Welche Gründe könnte es trotz Einsatz von Videokonferenzen für Geschäftsreisen geben?	

AUFGABE 7

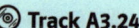 **Track A3.24**

Sie verfolgen eine englische Radiosendung zum Thema „Kleidung am Arbeitsplatz im Sommer".
Hören Sie aufmerksam zu und füllen Sie die folgende Tabelle auf Deutsch aus. Hören Sie sich den
Text zweimal an.

	Name	Alter / Nationalität	Beruf / Position	Unternehmen	Meinung / Erfahrung
1.	Michelle Lorraine				
2.	Lisa Best				
3.	Arne Singleton				
4.	Ed Richardson				
5.	Dave Parker				
6.	Peter Prescott				

Bearbeitungshinweise

- Bevor Sie beginnen, den Text zu lesen und Fragen zu beantworten, lesen Sie immer die Aufgabenstellung ganz durch.
- Markieren Sie die Schlüsselstellen in der Aufgabenstellung (z. B. Kreuzen Sie an …, Korrigieren Sie die falschen Aussagen, Nennen Sie Vorteile …).
- Lesen Sie nun den englischen Text und markieren Sie die Stellen, die Ihnen helfen die Fragen zu beantworten.
- Tragen Sie anschließend die Lösung in das Aufgabenblatt ein.
- Denken Sie daran, dass die Antworten immer auf Deutsch sind.
- Arbeiten Sie zügig, Sie verlieren sonst Zeit für die Beantwortung der anderen Prüfungsteile.
- In der Regel werden die Fragen im Text der Reihe nach beantwortet. Falls Sie noch eine Lücke haben, kann es sinnvoll sein, die Lösung zwischen der vorangegangen und der nachfolgenden markierten Textstelle zu suchen.

AUFGABE 1

Sie werden in einem Handelsunternehmen ausgebildet. Ihre Firma überlegt die Einführung der Möglichkeit auch mit Kreditkarte bezahlen zu können. Ergänzen Sie auf Seite 82 die hierzu fehlenden Informationen auf Deutsch.

Debit cards are king in the shops

For the first time, debit card spending in shops – including online shopping – has outstripped the use of cash.

Figures from the Association of Payment Clearing Services (Apacs) show that retail spending in the UK last year using debit cards rose by 9% to £89bn. Cash spending fell by 4% to £81bn, while credit card spending was unchanged at £61bn. Meanwhile the use of cheques continues to dwindle with only £9bn worth being written in shops.

Sandra Quinn of Apacs argued that many people and shops have got used to paying with plastic rather than cash, even for small items. "At the end of 2004, we saw total UK spending on plastic overtake cash for the first time, signalling a real sea change in our payment habits."

"This change was mainly driven by debit card use. The figures show that this trend is continuing with debit card spending in retail outlets crashing through the cash barrier for the first time ever," she added.

The Apacs figures highlight the rapid increase in the popularity of debit cards. First introduced more than 20 years ago, they have grown in use rapidly to overtake not only cheques but credit cards and now – in some circumstances – cash as well. They now account for 37% of all retail transactions.

Cash may be dwindling in popularity in shops and stores but is still widely used elsewhere. It is still more popular than any form of plastic when it comes to paying for travel tickets (such as train and bus fares), entertainment (for example, cinema and theatre tickets), payments to small businesses (such as plumbers) and for settling some bills.

Altogether cash to the value of £192bn was spent this way last year, compared with just £145bn using either debit or credit cards.

Quelle: BBC NEWS

A   Ergänzen Sie die Übersicht über den Einsatz der Zahlungsmittel. Kreuzen Sie an, was für das einzelne Zahlungsmittel zutrifft.

Zahlungsmittel	Anstieg	Rückgang	Einsatz unverändert

B   Beantworten Sie die folgenden Fragen zum Text auf Deutsch.

Nr.	Frage	Antwort
1.	Summe der Einzelhandelsumsätze mit Bankkarten	
2.	Änderungsrate beim Einsatz von Bargeld	
3.	Seit wann ist der Umsatz mit „Plastikgeld" größer als der mit Bargeld?	
4.	Welches Zahlungsmittel hat hauptsächlich zu diesem Wandel geführt?	
5.	Wie lange gibt es schon Bankkarten auf dem britischen Markt?	
6.	In welchen Fällen bezahlen Kunden weiterhin vorwiegend bar?	

AUFGABE 2

Travel perks trickle down to SMEs

DISCOUNTS, rewards and extras are no longer the preserve of corporate heavyweights as airlines wake up to the spending potential of small and medium-sized companies (SMEs).

More carriers are developing dedicated programmes to attract SMEs, offering them discounted fares and the chance to earn points in exchange for benefits, rewarding their loyalty in the same way a frequent-flyer scheme rewards an individual for his. Benefits include airport transfers, car hire, train tickets, hotel nights and lounge access.

Businesses can monitor their accounts and employees' travel patterns online, or the account can be managed by their travel management company. British Airways' corporate scheme, On Business, is open to any company with five or more travelling employees and without a BA corporate deal. This month it will allow the 14,000 companies registered to swap reward points for upgrades to redeem them online.

Scandinavian Airlines has published a guide to managing business travel aimed at SMEs and has a new online tool, the SAS travel adviser, for companies to identify their best products and services. Although single SMEs do not have the buying power of big companies, airlines see that their combined clout is huge. "SMEs are a growing market segment, with lots of largely unmanaged travel," says Thomas Brandt, Delta Airlines's general manager, distribution planning international.

"We want to support SMEs as they grow, then we can assist them with corporate deals," says Alan Lias, head of loyalty marketing for Virgin Atlantic, whose scheme, Flying Co, is open to companies with at least two travellers flying more than five round trips in qualifying classes to earn at least 20,000 core Flying Co miles a year.

BA claims to be the only airline that awards points to companies for all types of fares, even its cheapest, while other airlines give rewards only for "qualifying fares".

Car rental companies also run SME programmes. Hertz's Hertz Link offers corporate rates and free delivery and collection within a five-mile radius of its 136 locations. Budget Rent-a-Car's new Business Connections programme offers discounts, special offers and upgrades.

Hotels have been slower to tap in to the SME market. Starwood Hotels claims to be the only chain with a dedicated programme, Starwood Preferred Business, launched a year ago. Under this scheme, two starpoints are awarded to the traveller and one to the company for every dollar spent. Other benefits include upgraded rooms, late check out, and discounted rates.

Quelle: Times Online

Ihr Unternehmen unterhält mehrere überregionale und internationale Geschäftsbeziehungen. Sie haben obigen Artikel im Internet entdeckt und stellen nun die Informationen über die Angebote der Firmen speziell für kleine und mittlere Unternehmen auf Deutsch zusammen.

	Firma	Angebote
1.	**BA** „On Business"	
2.	**SAS**	
3.	**Virgin** „Flying Co"	
4.	**Hertz** „Hertz Link"	
5.	**Budget Rent-a-Car** „Business Connections"	
6.	**Starwood Hotels** „Starwood Preferred Business"	

AUFGABE 3

Ihre Chefin möchte für die Büroräume in der amerikanischen Niederlassung zehn Bücherregale kaufen. Sie interessiert sich für folgendes Angebot von HappyOffice24.com.

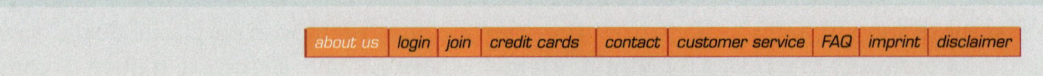

about us | login | join | credit cards | contact | customer service | FAQ | imprint | disclaimer

Office furniture
American Oak 72" High Bookcase

$198
List Price $259

Delivery $79
1–2 weeks for delivery
Ships by UPS

Add to Cart

IN-STOCK

Product Features
- Constructed of red oak solids and veneers
- Polyurethane finish resists stains
- Adjustable shelves edged with solid oak
- Bookcase shelves are 12" deep
- Ships ready to assemble
- FREE 5 Year Guarantee

Product Details	
Color:	Oak
Dimensions:	30"W x 12"D x 72"H
Weight (lbs):	98
Manufacturer:	Office Concepts

6-shelf bookcase is constructed of solid American Red Oak and genuine American Red Oak veneers on medium density fiberboard and has a polyurethane finish that resists stains. Adjustable shelves edged with solid oak compliment the beautiful solid oak molding.
Cam-lock construction for extra strength.
Assembly required.

Quantity Pricing

Item	1	2 and up
American Oak 72" High Bookcase	$198	$179

Merchandise Discounts

Order Subtotal	Merchandise Discount
$1500 – $2500	2% off
$2501 – $5000	4% off
$5001 – $9000	6% off
Over $9000	8% off

Volume Discounts

As your purchase volume increases, your order is eligible for Merchandise Discounts. Please see charts below. Your order total will be automatically recalculated as volume increases.

Shop Online! 24 Hours a Day, 7 Days a Week!
Place an order with our friendly sales staff:
1-800-933-0053
For service after the sale, **click here** or call:
1-800-933-0055
Hours: Mon – Fri 6:30 am – 9 pm,
Sat – Sun 8 am – 9 pm, Central Time

A Ergänzen Sie für Ihre Chefin die fehlenden Informationen in Deutsch.

1. Preis pro Stück

2. Lieferzeit

3. Lieferkosten

4. Versandart

5. Garantie

6. Farbe

7. Breite

8. Tiefe

9. Gewicht

10. Rabatt

11. Telefonnummer für den Kundenservice

12. Erreichbarkeit der Hotline

B Kreuzen Sie die richtige Antwort an.

	ja	nein	nicht genannt
1. vorrätig	☐	☐	☐
2. fertig montiert	☐	☐	☐
3. voll massiv	☐	☐	☐
4. automatischer Rabattabzug	☐	☐	☐
5. Zahlung auf Rechnung möglich	☐	☐	☐
6. Lieferant ist auch Hersteller	☐	☐	☐
7. Mailadresse: order@HappyOffice24.com	☐	☐	☐
8. Bestellung ausschließlich online möglich	☐	☐	☐

AUFGABE 4

Choosing the Best Structure for Your Business

There are four basic types of business entities: sole-proprietorships, partnerships, corporations, and limited liability companies, each with its own advantages and disadvantages. Consider these factors when choosing which is right for your business: tax aspects, legal requirements, and the potential for personal liability.

Sole-Proprietorship

A sole-proprietorship is a business that is owned by a single individual (or by a husband and wife) that is not a corporation or a limited liability company. There are no legal requirements to comply with in order to create and maintain the business structure. The biggest disadvantage is that you, the business owner, are held personally liable for the debts of the business. This means that if someone sues your business and obtains a judgement against it, you will be responsible for paying it even if it exceeds the entire worth of your business. You should evaluate the potential risk of this kind of liability for your type of business to determine whether you should operate as a corporation or limited liability company instead. An attorney who practices in the area of business law can help you make this determination and can also help you understand which business structure makes the most sense for you from a tax perspective.

Partnership

A partnership is a business that is owned by more than one individual (not a husband and wife) that is not a corporation or limited liability company. Nothing is required to establish the business as a partnership, it happens automatically when two or more people own a business that is not a corporation or a limited liability company. However, it is a good idea to have a written partnership agreement which spells out the commitments of the parties, including how much and what they will contribute to the business, how they will draw profits and share losses, and who will have authority and responsibility for making various decisions among other things. If the owners of the business do not make a written partnership agreement, state partnership law determines the obligations of the owners.

Corporation

A corporation can be owned by one or more individuals. Each state's laws spell out the requirements for setting up a corporation in that state. Generally, establishing a corporation involves drafting Articles of Incorporation and Bylaws and issuing stock. The Articles of Incorporation are filed with the State and a Certificate of Incorporation is issued to the business. The main advantage of operating a business as a corporation is that the liability of the owners for the debts of the corporation is limited to their investment in the business. The biggest disadvantage is that the business must adhere to the corporate structure by conducting shareholders and directors meetings, which can be cumbersome for a small business.

Limited Liability Company (LLC)

Each state's laws spell out the requirements for operating a business as a limited liability company. The basic structure of an LLC is that it combines the management aspects of a partnership with the liability advantage of a corporation. This makes it a very desirable structure for a business. However, like a corporation, there are legal requirements that must be met in order to preserve the status of the business as an LLC. Special care is also required in establishing the LLC to make sure the desired tax status is obtained. You should consult an attorney who practices business law to establish your limited liability company.

Quelle: AllLaw.com

Sie arbeiten in einem Unternehmen der IT-Branche. Ihr Unternehmen hat einige Kunden in den USA und möchte sich dort mit einem Tochterunternehmen niederlassen. Ihr Chef hat wenig Zeit und möchte sich schnell einen Überblick über die Merkmale verschiedener Rechtsformen verschaffen. Deshalb bittet er Sie die folgende Tabelle auszufüllen.

	Rechtsform	Personen-anzahl bei Gründung	gesetzliche Vorschriften bei Gründung	Haftung	Gesellschafts-vertrag	sonstige Vorteile und Nachteile
1.	Sole Proprietorship					
2.	Partnership					
3.	Corporation					
4.	Limited Liability Company (LLC)					

AUFGABE 5

Product piracy

It is the business crime wave of the 21st century. Product piracy is taking place on a worldwide scale and costs the European economy billions of euros every year.

The motive behind product piracy is easy to understand. Why invest in research and development when counterfeiting is so much easier? But it is hard to give an exact definition of the phenomenon. Experts agree that so-called "product piracy" infringes trade mark rights by using, for example, the Nike swoosh or the Lacoste crocodile in a commercial and criminal way. It encompasses not only the infringement of branded labels but also slightly modified imitations of branded goods. Such actions are committed in a purposeful, copious and profit-making manner.

According to the EU, 10% of world trade consists of fake products through product piracy, illegal overproduction and re-imports. This means annual economic damage on an international scale of 200–300 billion euros. The impact on companies is immense. Besides losses of sales and profits they also have to deal with damage to their company image and even, in the worst case, with product liability actions. Especially the new markets of producers of branded goods in Eastern Europe and Asia are imperilled by dramatic slumps in sales. Furthermore, copies which are inferior in quality to the originals cannot fulfil the expectations of the customers and so the reputation of the brand name may be irreparably damaged.

According to estimates of the German Ministry of Justice, about 50,000 jobs in Germany are lost yearly as a result of product piracy. Across Europe, approximately 300,000 jobs are affected. It is also assumed that profits made through the sale of fake products contribute to the financing of organised crime.

Basically, one can distinguish between three kinds of imitations:
1. The imitation's aim is to copy the original product 1:1. In this case, the packaging and brand name are usually identical. In the case of cosmetic and pharmaceutical products, even the ingredients may be the same.
2. In contrast to such "perfect" imitations, "classic" copies also have the same packaging and the same brand name but the ingredients are mostly inferior, non-existent or possibly even harmful.
3. The third kind of imitation is plagiarism, which normally uses a slightly modified brand name. The products sold under these names sometimes do not even exist in the range of the original brand name producer.

Many people are working intensively behind closed doors on solutions to the problem. Not only governments of EU member states but also the European Commission and, on a worldwide level, even the UN are all interested in finding a lasting solution.

From the point of view of the VBP, a German association which combats product piracy, co-operation is called for between the affected companies and their subsidiaries, licensees and other affected producers of branded goods. The affected industries must support the efforts of the authorities through concerted action. They cannot simply rely on stricter laws, controls and sanctions imposed by particular national governments or the EU to solve the problems of nationally organised product piracy.

By concentrating expert knowledge and efforts in the battle against product piracy, the required actions can be coordinated in a better way. This will allow improvement of data exchange on counterfeiters and so-called "piracy-centres", more efficient use of existing sources of information and the implementation of more successful defences. The VBP has also expressed the view that, in connection with such methods, an effective legal framework which accounts for trademark rights should be proactively implemented. The association already acts in the interests of its members by coordinating actions with national and European public authorities.

In terms of product safety, it is important to distinguish between identification features and security features. A logo, for example, is merely an identification feature, and can be easily imitated. It does not guarantee product safety. In contrast, a security feature is more difficult and complicated to copy, and is therefore more suitable for protecting products. For example, the technology already exists to allow proof of the originality of the product through a unique forgery-proof colour code, practically like a product fingerprint.

Sie arbeiten bei einem Markenartikelhersteller. In obigem Artikel in einer Fachzeitschrift hat eine englische Journalistin einen Gastbeitrag über Produktpiraterie geschrieben. Ihre Ausbilderin bittet Sie, ihr die folgenden Fragen zu dem Text auf Deutsch zu beantworten.

1. Wie wird der Begriff „Produktpiraterie" im Text beschrieben?

_____

_____

2. Wie setzen sich die 10 % des illegalen Handels zusammen?

_____

_____

3. Welche Auswirkungen hat dies für die Unternehmen und die Gesellschaft?

_____

_____

4. In welche drei Kategorien lassen sich Imitationen einteilen und wie unterscheiden sie sich?

_____

_____

_____

5. Wer beteiligt sich, eine Lösung zu finden, die Produktpiraterie in den Griff zu bekommen?

_____

_____

6. Wie sieht eine vernünftige Lösung aus Sicht der VBP aus?

_____

_____

7. Geben Sie jeweils ein Bespiel für Identifikationsmerkmale und Sicherheitsmerkmale.

_____

_____

Bearbeitungshinweise

Um englischsprachige Geschäftsbriefe korrekt erstellen zu können, ist es wichtig, die einzelnen Bestandteile und ihre Schreibweise zu kennen.

Inhalt	Schreibweise
Datum / Date Es gibt mehrere Möglichkeiten das Datum zu schreiben. Beispiel: 13. September 201_	13 September 201_ 13 September, 201_ 13th September 201_ 13th September, 201_ September 13, 201_ September 13th, 201_ **Tipp:** Merken Sie sich **eine** richtige Variante und benutzen Sie ausschließlich diese. Am einfachsten ist folgende Schreibweise: Tag Monat Jahr 13 September 2011 (ohne Zeichen dazwischen)
Reine Zahlenschreibweise: Beispiel: 03.08.2011	Hier muss zwischen britischem Englisch und amerikanischem Englisch unterschieden werden: British English: 03/08/11 (dd/mm/yyyy) American English: 08/03/11 (mm/dd/yyyy) **Tipp:** Um Missverständnisse zu vermeiden, ist es ratsam, den Monat auszuschreiben. Immer öfter wird auch folgende Schreibweise verwendet: 2011-08-03 (yyyy/mm/dd)
Anrede / Salutation und **Schlussformel / Complimentary close** Üblicherweise gehören Anrede und Schlussformel zusammen und hängen voneinander ab.	**Sie kennen die Person nicht:** Dear Sir or Madam / Dear Sirs → Yours sincerely → Yours faithfully **Sie kennen die Person:** Dear Mr / Mrs / Ms + Name der Person → Yours sincerely Bei E-Mails oder persönlichen Briefen (mit Anrede, z. B. Dear John) auch: → Kind regards → Best regards → Regards

Zeichensetzung / Punctuation

Nach Anrede und Schlussformel kann jeweils ein Komma gesetzt werden; die Kommasetzung muss für Anrede und Schlussformel einheitlich gehandhabt werden.	Dear Sir or Madam, **We** refer to … Yours sincerely, oder
Nach der Anrede wird groß geschrieben.	Dear Sir or Madam **We** refer to … Yours sincerely
Nach der Anrede *Mr / Mrs / Ms* kann ein Punkt gesetzt werden.	Dear Mr / Mrs / Ms + Name der Person oder Dear Mr./Mrs./Ms. + Name der Person
	Tipp: Merken Sie sich **eine** Variante und benutzen Sie ausschließlich diese. Am einfachsten ist es sich zu merken, **nichts** zu machen, d. h. keine Kommas bzw. Punkte zu setzen.

Betreff / Subject line

Wenn ein Betreff gewünscht ist wird dieser im britischen Englisch häufig nach der Anrede platziert, im amerikanischen Englisch oft auch vor der Anrede.	Your enquiry (BE)/inquiry (AE) dated … Re: Your enquiry (BE)/inquiry (AE) dated … **Re: Your enquiry (BE)/ inquiry (AE) dated …** Subject: Your enquiry (BE)/inquiry (AE) dated …
Man findet den Betreff häufig unterstrichen, fettgedruckt und / oder durch die Abkürzung **Re:** oder den Begriff **Subject:** eingeleitet.	**Hinweis:** Anrede und Bezug werden im Vergleich zum Deutschen häufig „umgedreht".

Unterschriftsblock / Signature block

Aufbau bei eigener Unterschrift: Handschriftliche Unterschrift Name gedruckt Position im Unternehmen	*Jane Miller* Jane Miller Sales Manager
Aufbau bei Unterschrift in fremdem Namen: Handschriftliche Unterschrift **for** Name der fremden Person Position im Unternehmen	*Ray Stokes* for Jane Miller Sales Manager

Anlagen / Enclosures

Auch hierfür findet man verschiedene Varianten.	**Eine Anlage** Enc Encl	**Mehrere Anlagen** Encs Encls
	oder	
Nach der Abkürzung kann ein Punkt gesetzt werden.	Enc. Encl.	Encs. Encls.

!

AUFGABE 1

Sie arbeiten in einem internationalen Konzern. Zur Zeit ist der amerikanische Produktionsleiter Dan Auber auf Rundreise und besucht die Werke in verschiedenen Ländern. Ihr Chef bittet Sie für Herrn Auber ein kurzes Anschreiben und einen Reiseplan in englischer Sprache für den weiteren Verlauf der Geschäftsreise zu erstellen. Verwenden Sie dazu die folgenden Angaben:

Infos für Weiterreise von Mr Auber

5. August
- Abflug: Flughafen Düsseldorf 9.10 Uhr, Ankunft: Shanghai 7.10 Uhr Ortszeit
- Unterkunft im Hilton Hotel Shanghai
- Abholung am Flughafen durch Herrn Yi Whang, Assistent der Geschäftsleitung
- 10 Uhr Besichtigung der Produktionstätten, anschließend Treffen mit der Geschäftsleitung und der Architektin zur Besprechung des Baus einer neuen Produktionshalle
- 19 Uhr gemeinsames Abendessen mit der Geschäftsführung und den Abteilungsleitern

6. August
- ganztägiger Besuch der Messe CHINAPLUS im Shanghai New International Expo Center (SNIEC)

7. August
- 9 Uhr Treffen mit Geschäftsleitung über weiteres Projektmanagement
- Abflug nach Chicago: 13.15 Uhr, Ankunft in Chicago: 22.20 Uhr Ortszeit

AUFGABE 2

Verfassen Sie eine E-Mail in englischer Sprache an das Santa Fe Inn in Santa Fe, New Mexico, da Sie für eine bevorstehende Geschäftsreise noch Hotelzimmer buchen und weitere Dinge klären müssen. Verwenden Sie dazu folgende Angaben:

- Buchen Sie zwei Einzelzimmer mit Bad; Zeitraum: 25. bis 31. Mai dieses Jahres.
- Der hoteleigene Abholservice vom Flughafen wird gerne in Anspruch genommen; genaue Ankunftszeit wird rechtzeitig bekannt gegeben.
- Für den 28. Mai wird der Konferenzraum des Hotels für ein Treffen mit den Geschäftspartnern gebucht; Flipchart und Beamer werden benötigt.
- Während des Geschäftstreffens soll für Getränke und einen kleinen Imbiss gesorgt werden, anschließend werden die Gäste zum Abendessen ins hoteleigene Restaurant eingeladen, daher Bitte um Zusendung einiger Menüvorschläge.
- Finden Sie einen angemessenen Schlusssatz.

From:	(your e-mail address)
To:	SantaFeInn@hotel.usa
Sent:	(today's date)
Subject:	

AUFGABE 3

Sie werden von Ihrer Chefin gebeten, eine Anfrage in englischer Sprache an die Firma Tech Ltd. in Manchester / UK zu schreiben. Folgende Punkte sollen Sie klären:

- Nehmen Sie Bezug auf die Anzeige in der letzten Ausgabe der Fachzeitschrift *Technology Trends*.
- Ihr Unternehmen vertreibt elektronische Bauteile, die es Ihren Kunden ermöglichen, sich Computer nach eigenen Bedürfnissen zusammenzustellen. In Deutschland sind Sie Marktführer.
- Fragen Sie nach dem aktuellen Katalog und der Preisliste.
- Erkundigen Sie sich auch nach den Liefer- und Zahlungsbedingungen sowie der Lieferzeit.
- Beenden Sie die E-Mail in angemessener Weise.

```
From:     (your e-mail address)
To:       info@tech.ltd.com
Sent:     (today's date)
Subject:  Request for catalogue and price list
```

AUFGABE 4

Sie werden gebeten für den Tag der offenen Tür Ihres Unternehmens einen Flyer in englischer Sprache zu entwerfen. Hierzu erhalten Sie von Ihrem Ausbilder folgende Informationen zum Ablauf des Tages:

- „auffallende" Überschrift
- Tag der offenen Tür am 17. Mai auf dem Firmengelände in Schwabach
- Besichtigungen der neuen Produktionshalle und der Labore
- Führungen über das Gelände, stündlich in Englisch und Deutsch
- Filmvorführungen auch in Spanisch und Französisch
- buntes Kinderprogramm (überlegen Sie sich zwei Programmpunkte)
- Essen und Getränke frei
- angemessener Schlusssatz (z. B. Aufforderung zum Vorbeikommen)

AUFGABE 5

Sie werden von Ihrem Abteilungsleiter gebeten, einen kurzen Newsletter in englischer Sprache an alle Kunden und Lieferanten zu senden, in dem Sie zu Ihrem jährlichen Tag der offenen Tür einladen. Folgende Punkte sollen erwähnt werden:

- Tag der offenen Tür findet am 13. April dieses Jahres auf dem Gelände des Unternehmens statt.
- Das neue Verwaltungsgebäude und die Labore können besichtigt werden.
- Es gibt stündlich Führungen über das Gelände, die in Französisch, Spanisch und Deutsch gehalten werden.
- Auch Kinder sind herzlich willkommen. Es gibt ein spezielles Programm mit unterschiedlichsten Aktivitäten.
- Die verbindliche Anmeldung sollte bis zum 31. März erfolgen.
- Beenden Sie den Newsletter in angemessener Weise.

AUFGABE 6

Sie sind bei der Firma Büro Aktuell KG in der Ausbildung. Ihre Vorgesetzte bittet Sie die Bestellungen zu bearbeiten und Auftragsbestätigungen zu versenden. Dies geschieht in der Firma per E-Mail. Formulieren Sie eine E-Mail in englischer Sprache an Kate Duncan von der Firma Paper Ltd. in Glasgow mit folgendem Inhalt:

- Nehmen Sie Bezug auf die Bestellung vom 5. Juni dieses Jahres mit der Auftragsnummer 2987.
- Bestätigen Sie die Bestellung der 1.500 Briefumschläge und der 250 Aktenordner.
- Die bestellten 20 Drehstühle können momentan nicht in der gewünschten Anzahl geliefert werden; 10 Stühle sind noch vorrätig (Lieferung innerhalb einer Woche), die restlichen können erst in 6 Wochen geliefert werden.
- Bei Einverständnis mit diesem Vorschlag bitte Bestätigung per E-Mail schicken.
- Finden Sie einen angemessenen Schlusssatz.

From:	(your name)@Buero.aktuell.de
To:	MsDuncan@paper-ltd.co.uk
Sent:	(today's date)
Subject:	

AUFGABE 7

Sie arbeiten in der Buchhaltung der Firma Fuchs GmbH und sollen heute eine zweite Zahlungs-erinnerung an Herrn McAllister von der Firma Dean Corp. versenden. Bislang hat dieses Unternehmen die Rechnungen fristgerecht bezahlt. Verwenden Sie folgende Angaben:

- Nehmen Sie Bezug auf die Rechnung vom 30. August dieses Jahres; Rechnungsnummer 038/1898-F, Rechnungsbetrag: 4.798,00 EUR, Fälligkeit: 30. September dieses Jahres.
- Verweisen Sie auf die erste Zahlungserinnerung vom 5. Oktober dieses Jahres.
- Geschäftsbeziehung besteht seit über 10 Jahren und bisher wurden Rechnungen immer fristgerecht bezahlt.
- Bestehen Sie auf Überweisung des Betrags bis zum 15. Oktober dieses Jahres.
- Falls die Zahlung nicht erfolgt, sehen Sie sich gezwungen gerichtliche Schritte einzuleiten.
- Sollte die Rechnung schon beglichen worden sein, so soll diese Zahlungserinnerung als gegenstandslos betrachtet werden.

```
From:     (your name)@fuchs.de
To:       McAllister@DeanCorp.com
Sent:     201_-10-12
Subject:
```

AUFGABE 8

Sie arbeiten beim Fahrradgroßhandel Tulip OHG in Köln und sollen im Auftrag Ihres Chefs eine Bestellung per E-Mail in englischer Sprache aufgeben, damit beim Start in die neue Saison ausreichend Ware vorhanden ist. Folgende Punkte sind zu berücksichtigen:

- Nehmen Sie Bezug auf den aktuellen Frühjahrskatalog, den Sie kürzlich erhalten haben.
- Nennen Sie die Auftragsnummer 85297 und die Artikel, die Sie bestellen möchten: 200 Sättel (Artikelnummer: 24, Einzelpreis: 24,95 EUR), 220 Lenker (Artikelnummer: 88, Einzelpreis: 55,00 EUR), 300 Tachometer (Artikelnummer: 69, Einzelpreis: 16,50 EUR) und 80 Packtaschen (Artikelnummer: 56, Einzelpreis: 80,00 EUR).
- Sie gehen davon aus, dass die Lieferbedingungen die gleichen sind wie bei Ihrer letzten Bestellung, nämlich frachtfrei, und dass die Lieferung innerhalb von zwei Wochen nach Bestellung eintreffen wird.
- Die Bezahlung erfolgt nach Erhalt der Ware rein netto.
- Drücken Sie aus, dass Sie bei gutem Absatz der Ware gerne weitere Aufträge erteilen würden.

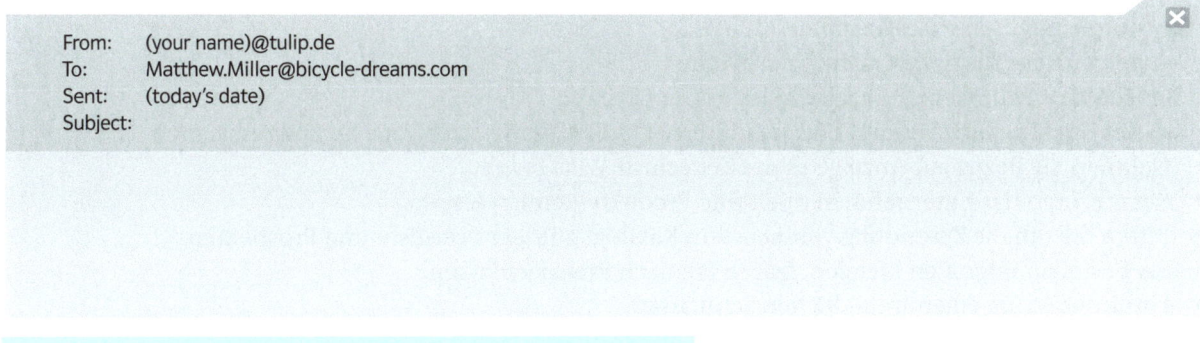

```
From:     (your name)@tulip.de
To:       Matthew.Miller@bicycle-dreams.com
Sent:     (today's date)
Subject:
```

Lenker – handle bar; Tachometer – speedometer; Packtasche – pannier

AUFGABE 9

Sie arbeiten bei einem Großhändler für Büroausstattung und Bürozubehör. Ihre Chefin bittet Sie ein Fax für Ihren Stammkunden Top Furniture in Irland über folgende Rabattaktion zu verfassen:

Abverkauf Fine Design

- Ausverkauf der exklusiven Büromöbelserie Fine Design wegen Herstellerwechsel
- bis zu 70 % Rabatt auf alle Möbel
- Gratisversand innerhalb von 3 Werktagen (10 Tage EU-Ausland, 14 Tage Rest) ab 500 Euro Bestellwert
- Hinweis, dass bei jeder Bestellung die Nummer der Sonderaktion 5665 angegeben werden muss
- kein Mindestbestellwert
- 14-tägige Sonderaktion nur für Stammkunden
- angemessener Schlusssatz mit Hinweis, dass sich die Kunden diese Aktion auf keinen Fall entgehen lassen sollten

Büromarkt Mauerstraße 12 40547 Düsseldorf	Tel.: +49 211 581923 Fax: +49 211 581924 www.FineDesign.com

Telefax Message

To:	Top Furniture 86 Greenhill Road Dublin 2, Ireland	**Attention:** Mrs Smyth	
		Fax: +353 1 798 9523	
From:			
Date:		**Pages:** (incl. this page) 1	
Subject:			

AUFGABE 10

Sie arbeiten bei einem Weingroßhändler in Deutschland, der eine größere Menge kalifornischer Weine aus den USA importieren möchte. Aus diesem Grund hat Ihr Vorgesetzter Sie gebeten folgende Anfrage in englischer Sprache zu verfassen. Ihre Aufgabe ist es, einen Brieftext einschließlich Anrede und Schlussformel zu erstellen.

- Stellen Sie das Unternehmen vor:
  - mittelständischer Großhändler
  - bekannt für die hohe Qualität der Weine
  - Lieferant zahlreicher Einzelhändler in Deutschland
  - seit Kurzem auch Verkauf über das Internet, daher große Nachfrage an Spitzenweinen
- Nehmen Sie Bezug auf Anzeige in der Zeitschrift *Wine Today*.
- Sie möchten das Unternehmen und seine Produkte kennen lernen.
- Bitten Sie um die Zusendung von neustem Katalog, gültiger Preisliste und Prospekten.
- Sie bestellen in großen Mengen, fragen Sie nach Preisnachlässen.
- Formulieren Sie einen freundlichen Schlusssatz.

AUFGABE 11

Sie arbeiten bei der Firma SmartPack GmbH, die Verpackungsmaterialien aller Art für den globalen Markt herstellt. Sie haben mit einem Kunden einen Kaufvertrag abgeschlossen und möchten ihm nun eine Versandanzeige für die Ware senden. Verfassen Sie das Schreiben in englischer Sprache nach folgenden Angaben einschließlich Anrede und Schlussformel:

- Anrede: Ms Gregori
- Nehmen Sie Bezug auf die Bestellung Nr. 3456-208 vom 5. Februar dieses Jahres.
- Teilen Sie Folgendes mit:
  - die bestellte Ware ist auf Lager und zum sofortigen Versand bereit
  - wie vereinbart wird die Ware per Luftfracht versandt
- Wie gewünscht wurde die Ware in Kisten verpackt und mit der Liefernummer versehen.
- Folgende Lieferdokumente wurden unserer Bank übergeben:
  - unterschriebene Handelsrechnung dreifach
  - Luftfrachtbrief
  - Ursprungszeugnis
- Bitte um Benachrichtigung sobald die Ware angekommen ist.
- Finden Sie einen freundlichen Schlusssatz.

AUFGABE 12

Sie arbeiten in der Einkaufabteilung der Firma Fashion Luxury GmbH, einem Großhändler für Damen- und Herrenbekleidung. Ihr Unternehmen hat bei einem Hersteller in New York ein Angebot eingeholt, auf das Sie nun in einem Schreiben reagieren. Sie haben bisher mit dem Hersteller noch keine Geschäfte getätigt. Ihre Aufgabe ist es, einen Brieftext in englischer Sprache einschließlich Anrede und Schlussformel nach folgenden Angaben zu erstellen:

- Anrede: Mr Hartlieb
- Bezugszeile: Angebot Nr. 786/ZZ vom 14. April dieses Jahres
- Danken Sie für das Angebot, aber Sie haben noch Fragen:
  - Aus welchem Material sind die Hosen (Artikelnr. T 23)?
  - Welche Farbkombination haben die Anzüge (Artikelnr. S 56)?
  - Fragen Sie nach einem Farbmuster für obige Anzüge.
- Fragen Sie nach dem neuen Herbstkatalog.
- Bitten Sie um eine genaue Auskunft über die Liefer- und Zahlungsbedingungen.
- Finden Sie einen freundlichen Schlusssatz.
- Beenden Sie den Brief mit Ihrer eigenen Unterschrift und Ihrer Position im Unternehmen.

AUFGABE 13

Sie arbeiten bei der Schmidt GmbH, einem Großhändler für Textilien aller Art. Die Schmidt GmbH hat bei einem ausländischen Hersteller verschiedene Textilien eingekauft und geliefert bekommen, allerdings war die Sendung nicht zu Ihrer Zufriedenheit. Ihr Chef im Einkauf, Herr Helmut Koller, bittet Sie nun einen Beschwerdebrief in englischer Sprache nach untenstehenden Angaben zu verfassen.
Ihre Aufgabe ist es, einen Brieftext einschließlich Anrede, Schlussformel und Unterschriftsblock zu erstellen.

- Nehmen Sie Bezug auf die Bestellung Nr. R 205-145 vom 25. März dieses Jahres.
- Die Ware wurde heute geliefert und ist nicht zu unserer Zufriedenheit ausgefallen.
- Beim Überprüfen der Ware wurden folgende Mängel lt. Liste festgestellt:

Bestellte Ware	Fehler
Tischtücher (TC 30) 10 Stück, Größe 130 cm x 200 cm	zwei Tücher waren verschmutzt, da die Verpackung beschädigt war
Handtücher (TW 05) 15 Stück, Größe 100 cm x 180 cm	falsche Farbe: bestellt gelb, geliefert grün
Kissen (PI 02) 20 Stück, Größe 30 cm x 30 cm	5 Kissen sind ohne Latexfüllung 5 weitere Kissen haben Baumwollüberzug, bestellt war Seidenüberzug

- Ware wurde speziell bestellt, um unser Lager aufzufüllen, daher keine Verwendung für die gesendete Ware.
- Vorschlag: Ware wird zu Lasten des Lieferanten zurückgeschickt; wir wünschen Ersatz wie ursprünglich bestellt.
- Formulieren Sie einen freundlichen Schlusssatz und unterschreiben Sie den Brief im Namen von Herrn Koller.

AUFGABE 14

Sie arbeiten bei der Firma Puppen Maier GmbH, die handgefertigte Puppen für den ausländischen Markt herstellt. Einer Ihrer Kunden hat seine offene Rechnung noch nicht beglichen. Schreiben Sie eine erste Mahnung in englischer Sprache gemäß folgender Angaben Ihrer Chefin. Beginnen Sie Ihren Brief mit der Anrede und unterschreiben Sie selbst.

- Ansprechpartner: Herr Morgan
- Nehmen Sie Bezug auf unsere Rechnung Nr. 06-12-05 vom 25. Mai dieses Jahres über einen Betrag von € 3.250,00.
- Die Rechnung war am 25. Juni dieses Jahres fällig.
- Vielleicht hat der Kunde die Rechnung übersehen?
- Die Geschäftsbeziehung besteht schon seit mehreren Jahren und alle Rechnungen wurden bisher umgehend bezahlt.
- Bitten Sie um Begleichung der Rechnung.
- Falls Rechnung in der Zwischenzeit beglichen wurde, ist dieses Schreiben gegenstandslos.
- Nutzen Sie die Gelegenheit den Kunden auf den aktuellen Katalog und die neue Preisliste hinzuweisen.
- Anlässlich unseres 25-jährigen Firmenjubiläums gewähren wir auf alle handgefertigten Puppen einen Sonderrabatt von 10 %.
- Formulieren Sie einen freundlichen Schlusssatz und verweisen Sie auf die Anlagen: Kopie der Rechnung, Katalog und Preisliste.

AUFGABE 15

Sie arbeiten bei der Firma Sunrays KG, die Trockenfrüchte aller Art produziert und vertreibt. Ihr Vorgesetzter beauftragt Sie die Bestellung der Firma Healthy Dieting Ltd auf Englisch zu bestätigen. Die nötigen Informationen entnehmen Sie bitte der nachstehenden Notiz. Ihre Aufgabe ist es, einen Brieftext einschließlich Anrede und Schlussformel zu erstellen.

- Danken Sie für die Bestellung Nr. SR 1212-06 vom 22. März dieses Jahres.
- Bestätigen Sie wie folgt:
  - 100 Pakete Ananasringe, ohne Zuckerzusatz, zum Preis von jeweils 4,50 EUR.
  - Aufgrund der hohen Stückzahl bei den Ananasringen gewähren wir einen Mengenrabatt von 5 %.
  - 50 Pakete gemischte rote Früchte, bestehend aus Erdbeere, Himbeere, Preiselbeere, zum Preis von jeweils 6,30 EUR.
  - 20 Pakete getrocknete Pflaumen, sind im Moment aufgrund einer großen Nachfrage nicht auf Lager und werden nachgeliefert sobald das Lager wieder gefüllt ist.
  - Wir werden den Kunden unverzüglich davon benachrichtigen.
- Wie vereinbart, wird die restliche Ware bis zum Ende der Woche geliefert.
- Finden Sie einen freundlichen Schlusssatz, der den Wunsch nach weiteren Geschäftsbeziehungen ausdrückt.

AUFGABE 16

Sie lesen diese Anzeige in der *Financial Times*. Verfassen Sie ein Bewerbungsschreiben mit nachfolgendem Inhalt. Ihre Aufgabe ist es einen vollständigen Brieftext in englischer Sprache zu verfassen, beginnend mit der Anrede.

- Formulieren Sie einen geeigneten Betreff.
- Nehmen Sie Bezug auf die Stellenanzeige vom 15. August dieses Jahres und bekunden Sie Interesse an der ausgeschriebenen Stelle.
- Ihre derzeitige berufliche Position: Assistent/-in des Verkaufsleiters bei der Firma Friedrich Berger GmbH, einem mittelständischen Unternehmen im Dienstleistungssektor.
- Ihr Aufgabengebiet umfasst: Neukundengewinnung, Vertragsabschlüsse und Pflege der Kundenbeziehungen.
- Sie arbeiten dort schon 3 Jahre und suchen eine neue berufliche Herausforderung im europäischen Ausland.
- Bringen Sie zum Ausdruck, dass Sie ein geeigneter Bewerber sind:
  - Sie sind sehr organisiert, flexibel und können im Team arbeiten.
  - Sie haben sehr gute Englischkenntnisse.
- Der Geschäftsführer der Friedrich Berger GmbH steht für Referenzen zur Verfügung.
- Schließen Sie den Brief angemessen und unterschreiben Sie.
- Anlage: Lebenslauf

Sales Coordinator
Position based in Manchester, UK

We are looking for an enthusiastic, focused and well-organised individual to be a welcome addition to our sales team for the Manchester location. You must be committed to winning and working hard in a team sales environment. The Sales Coordinator's primary focus will be service support. This person should be extremely organised, responsible, and should work well within a group.

Please send a current version of your CV to InterCo plc with the subject line: Sales Coordinator – Manchester

Your application will not be considered if the subject of your letter is incorrect.

AUFGABE 17

Sie machen ein Auslandspraktikum bei der Firma Garden Paradise Ltd. in Exeter, GB, die Gartenmöbel aller Art für internationale Kunden vertreibt. Der Leiter der Verkaufsabteilung bittet Sie eine Anfrage gemäß den folgenden Angaben auf Englisch zu beantworten. Ihre Aufgabe ist es einen Brieftext einschließlich Anrede und Schlussformel zu erstellen.

- Ansprechpartner: Mr Jamahomi, Bezug auf die Anfrage vom 15. Februar dieses Jahres
- Danken Sie für das Interesse an unserer neuen Produktpalette.
- Folgendes Angebot können wir unterbreiten:
  - Gartenmöbel Relax (Katalognummer R34) ist in den Farbkombinationen blau-grau und schwarz-violett erhältlich.
  - Die Gartenbank Holiday (Katalognummer B34) ist in zwei Größen (mit 2 oder 4 Sitzen) erhältlich, die Kissen dazu sind im Preis enthalten.
  - Heben Sie den günstigen Gesamtpreis für eine Bank und Möbel hervor, die im Set nur £ 499,00 kosten.
  - Der Kunde spart gegenüber dem Normalpreis 15 %.
- Für Neukunden gelten folgende Liefer- und Zahlungsbedingungen:
  - Die im Katalog genannten Preise beinhalten Kosten, Versicherung und Fracht (CIP).
  - Wir gewähren ein Zahlungsziel von 30 Tagen nach Datum der Rechnung.
- Erwähnen Sie im Brieftext folgende Anlage: unser neuster Sommerkatalog, dem weitere Details entnommen werden können.
- Finden Sie einen freundlichen Schlusssatz.

AUFGABE 18

Sie arbeiten in der Einkaufsabteilung der Firma Globetraveller GmbH in Karlsruhe, die Outdoorartikel aller Art vertreibt. Ihre Chefin bittet Sie, anhand der nachstehenden Vorgaben, bei der englischen Firma Leisure World Ltd. in Peterborough, North Lincolnshire, LN3 4BJ, Great Britain, eine Bestellung vorzunehmen. Verfassen Sie das komplette Schreiben unterschriftsreif für Ihre Chefin, Lioba Blüm, in englischer Sprache. Ihr Zeichen ist MM, Ihre Durchwahl 0721 / 7135-212. Verwenden Sie den dafür vorgesehenen Briefvordruck.

- Betreff: Unsere Bestellung Nr. 12789-65
- Danken Sie für das Angebot mit Katalog und aktueller Preisliste.
- Bestellen Sie folgende Artikel:
  - Walking Boots Columbia Lady, aus wasserdichtem Leder, jeweils 3 Paar in Größe 37–41
  - Nordic Jacket Men, wasser- und windabweisend, Farbe titanium/schwarz, jeweils 2 Paar in Größe M–XL
  - 3 Zelte Happy Family, Großzelt für maximal 6 Personen, Farbe grün/silber, Gewicht 10kg
- Wir bestellen zu den in der aktuellen Preisliste angegebenen Preisen mit einem Einführungsrabatt von 5%.
- Bitten Sie darum, dass die Ware sorgfältig in Kisten verpackt wird, die durchnummeriert und mit einem roten Kreis gekennzeichnet werden.
- Weisen Sie darauf hin, dass die Ware bis spätestens 30 Tage nach der Bestellung bei uns eingegangen sein muss.
- Bitten Sie um eine Bestätigung des Liefertermins.
- Finden Sie einen angemessenen Schlusssatz und eine passende Grußformel.

Globetraveller GmbH

Kaiserstrasse 76, 75013 Karlsruhe
Tel. 0721-7134, Fax 0721-7135
www.globetraveller-karlsruhe.de

Globetraveller GmbH   Kaiserstrasse 76   75013 Karlsruhe

Ihr Zeichen	Unser Zeichen	Telefon	Datum

AUFGABE 19

Sie arbeiten für die Firma H&G Gerlach GmbH, einem Lederspezialist in Pirmasens, dessen Kennzeichen seit mehr als 100 Jahren die Herstellung von hochwertigen handgefertigten Schuhen ist. Garfield Shoes Ltd., 60 Main Road, London W1X 4DD, hat Ihrer Firma eine Anfrage über handgefertigte Herrenschuhe geschickt. Verfassen Sie für Ihren Chef, den Verkaufsleiter Helmut Gerlach, der den Brief selbst unterschreiben wird, ein Angebot an die Einkaufsleiterin von Garfield Shoes Ltd., Frau Mary Taylor (Zeichen MaTa). Als Vorlage erhalten Sie die untenstehenden Angaben. Verfassen Sie einen vollständigen Brief, der in der äußeren Form englischen bzw. amerikanischen Gepflogenheiten entspricht. Verwenden Sie den dafür vorgesehenen Briefvordruck.

- Datum 12. Oktober dieses Jahres, Ihr Zeichen, Durchwahl -563
- Nehmen Sie Bezug auf die Anfrage vom 5. Oktober dieses Jahres über handgefertigte Herrenschuhe, Größe 39–44.
- Erläutern Sie unsere Geschäftätigkeit und heben Sie besonders hervor, dass unsere Schuhe aus hochwertigem Leder zu wettbewerbsfähigen Preisen hergestellt werden.
- Wir gewähren folgende Rabatte:
  - Mengenrabatt von 5 % bei großen Bestellungen (ab 500 Paar Schuhen)
  - Einführungsrabatt von 10 % für Erstaufträge, um die Produkte auf dem britischen Markt zu platzieren
- Üblicherweise gelten folgende Zahlungsbedingungen:
  - Zahlung durch unwiderrufliches Dokumentenakkreditiv bei Erstaufträgen; wenn sich die Geschäftsbeziehung stabilisiert hat, können die Zahlungsmodalitäten neu verhandelt werden
  - Alle Preise sind FCA Pirmasens einschließlich der Exportkosten
- Verweisen Sie auf unseren neusten Katalog und die Exportpreisliste als Anlage.
- Heben Sie unser neustes Modell ComfyStyle hervor (Seite 13 im Katalog), das auf der Schuhmesse in Mailand sehr erfolgreich war. Qualität und modisches Design werden hier mit hohem Tragekomfort verbunden.
- Für weitere Fragen stehen wir gerne zur Verfügung.
- Finden Sie eine freundliche Schlussformel.

Der Lederspezialist

H&G Gerlach GmbH
Am Westpark 49
66953 Pirmasens
Telefon: 06331-857   Fax: 06331-853
www.gerlach-leder.de

H&G Gerlach GmbH   Am Westpark 49   66953 Pirmasens

Ihr Zeichen	Unser Zeichen	Telefon	Datum

Bearbeitungshinweise

- Streben Sie keine wörtliche Übersetzung an. Die Übersetzung sollte sinngemäß sein!
- Suchen Sie nach grammatikalisch einfachen und Ihnen bekannten Formulierungen.
- Schlagen Sie nicht jedes Wort nach. Dadurch verlieren Sie zu viel Zeit. Es ist wichtiger die Aufgabe vollständig zu bearbeiten.
- Vorsicht bei Dezimalzahlen:
  - Die Dezimalstelle wird im Englischen mit Punkt abgetrennt, im Deutschen mit Komma:
    Beispiel: Englisch   3.5 (= three point five)
              Deutsch   3,5 (= drei Komma fünf)
  - Die Hunderterstellen werden im Deutschen mit Punkt abgetrennt, im Englischen mit Komma:
    Beispiel: Englisch   300,000 (= three hundred thousand)
              Deutsch   300.000 (= Dreihunderttausend)
- Vorsicht bei großen Zahlen:

Deutsch	British English	American English	Achtung:	
Million	million	million	An *billion / million* wird kein Plural -s angehängt:	
Milliarde	thousand million	billion	drei Millionen Dollar	three million dollars
Billion	billion	trillion	zwei Milliarden Jahre	two billion years
			Ausnahme: Milliarden von Dollar	billions of dollars

!

Mediation: Textwiedergabe in englischer Sprache

AUFGABE 1

Im Rahmen Ihrer Ausbildung sind Sie in der Marketing Abteilung. Dort sind zwei Praktikanten aus Australien, für die Sie ein Merkblatt für den richtigen Ablauf von Kundenbefragungen ins Englische übertragen.

Checkliste für Kundenbefragungen
- Gehen Sie freundlich auf den zu befragenden Kunden zu.
- Stellen Sie sich selbst und das Unternehmen vor.
- Erklären Sie dem Kunden das Ziel und den Grund unserer Befragung.
- Stellen Sie alle Fragen, in der vorgegebenen Reihenfolge.
- Geben Sie dem Kunden genug Zeit über die Antwort nachzudenken.
- Kommentieren Sie die Antworten des Kunden nicht!
- Halten Sie die Antworten sofort im Fragebogen fest.
- Lassen Sie sich nicht in ein persönliches Gespräch verwickeln.
- Danken Sie dem Kunden für seine Mitwirkung und verabschieden Sie sich freundlich.

AUFGABE 2

Sie sind bei der Firma Globetech beschäftigt, einem weltweit expandierenden deutschen Technologieunternehmen, das Werbeanzeigen in ausländischen Zeitungen platzieren möchte, um internationalen Kunden das Unternehmen vorzustellen. Übertragen Sie die Inhalte der deutschen Anzeige in die englische Sprache.

Wir über uns

· im März 2002 in Hamburg gegründet
· seither rasant gewachsen
· in den letzten drei Jahren Niederlassungen in Großbritannien, den Niederlanden, Österreich und Russland eröffnet

Produkte

Das Sortiment umfasst Scanner, Projektoren, Notebooks, Tastaturen, Monitore und Digitalkameras sowie Lösungen für mobile Kommunikation.

Service

· Service Hotlines rund um die Uhr die ganze Woche besetzt
· Fachpersonal kann für fast jedes Problem Lösungen bieten

Stellenangebote

· Immer auf der Suche nach neuen Mitarbeitern mit Interesse an einer neuen Herausforderung.
· Suchen Sie einen Arbeitsplatz?
· Bitte senden Sie uns Ihren Lebenslauf per Post.
· Wir freuen uns auf Ihre Bewerbung.

AUFGABE 3

Sie arbeiten in einem Großhandel für Büroausstattung. Ihr Unternehmen stellt seine Produkte und Dienstleistungen auf einer Messe für Büroartikel aus. Zu diesem Zweck wurden Sie gebeten, die Inhalte einer PowerPoint Präsentation in die englische Sprache zu übertragen.

Alles fürs Büro zu Sparpreisen!

Von Büromöbeln bis zur Bürotechnik, vom Schreibtisch zum EDV-Zubehör alles aus einer Hand.

Nutzen Sie die verschiedenen Möglichkeiten zu bestellen:

– direkt in einem Fachgeschäft oder
– über das Internet

Nutzen Sie auch die verschiedenen Möglichkeiten Geld zu sparen:

– durch wöchentlich wechselnde Rabatte auf ausgewählte Produkte
– kostenlose Versendung bei Bestellwert über 99 Euro
– werden Sie Mitglied im SavingsClub und erhalten Sie spezielle Angebote und Gutscheine

Fragen Sie unsere Mitarbeiter nach speziellen Messeangeboten.

Übrigens: Wir helfen unserer Umwelt – wir recyceln unsere Produkte unentgeltlich!

AUFGABE 4

Sie arbeiten bei einem Messeveranstalter, der einen Informationstag für Berufseinsteiger organisiert. Ihre Aufgabe ist es, die Informationen eines Flyers in die englische Sprache zu übertragen, damit auch ein internationales Publikum erreicht werden kann.

- Finden Sie eine geeignete Überschrift.
- Informationsveranstaltung, die sich an Schüler, Auszubildende und Studenten richtet, mit Abschluss in den nächsten zwei Jahren.
- Sie erhalten aktuelle Informationen zu
  – verschiedenen Ausbildungsberufen in der Industrie- und Dienstleistungsbranche
  – Berufs- und Karrierechancen des jeweiligen Berufs.
- An zahlreichen Messeständen stellen sich Unternehmen aus ganz Deutschland vor.
- Ausbilder und Personalleiter stehen jederzeit für Fragen zur Verfügung.
- Einmalige Chance, persönliche Kontakte mit Personalleitung zu knüpfen – ein Vorteil bei einer späteren Bewerbung.
- Weiteres Angebot: verschiedene Vorträge rund um das Thema Bewerbung.
- Eintritt 6,00 Euro inklusive Essensgutschein.

AUFGABE 5

Sie arbeiten bei der KomTech GmbH und sind zuständig für die Erstellung eines Flyers für eine Messe in Großbritannien. Folgende Geschäftsinformationen gilt es in die englische Sprache zu übertragen:

- KomTech: Ein weltweites Unternehmen, das im wachsenden Markt der Mobilfunkkommunikation eine führende Position einnimmt.
- Ein Pionier im Bereich der Mobiltelefonie.
- KomTech liefert darüber hinaus Lösungen und Produkte für mobile Datenkommunikation.
- Für viele Unternehmen ist es eine Herausforderung, Produkte für diesen zukunftsorientierten Markt zu produzieren. Wir bei KomTech stellen uns dieser Herausforderung Tag für Tag.
- Fakten und Zahlen:
  – Produktionsstätten in 7 Ländern auf 3 Kontinenten
  – Forschungs- und Entwicklungszentren in 14 Ländern auf 4 Kontinenten
  – jeder dritte Mitarbeiter von KomTech arbeitet in Forschung und Entwicklung
  – über 60.000 Mitarbeiter auf der ganzen Welt
  – Verkauf von Mobiltelefonen in 70 Ländern
- KomTech in Deutschland:
  – Deutschland einer der wichtigsten Märkte von KomTech weltweit
  – Nettoumsatz im laufenden Geschäftsjahr in Deutschland insgesamt 1,679 Milliarden Euro

AUFGABE 6

Sie arbeiten bei SCE in der Marketing Abteilung und sind zuständig für die Erstellung eines Flyers für ausländische Besuchergruppen. Folgende Geschäftsinformationen gilt es sinngemäß in die englische Sprache zu übertragen.

Willkommen bei SCE – einem der größten Elektronik Unternehmen der Welt
- Wir sind ein globales Unternehmen, das seit Jahren in über 190 Ländern vertreten ist.
- Mehr als 49.000 Mitarbeiter arbeiten in Forschung und Entwicklung.
- Unser jährliches Bruttobudget übersteigt 5 Milliarden Euro.
- SCE ist ein höchst innovatives Unternehmen – 80 Prozent unserer Produkte wurden in den letzten 5 Jahren entwickelt.
- SCE – Ihr weltweiter Partner! Wir erfüllen alle Ihre Wünsche!
- In unserem Onlineshop können Sie direkt 24 Stunden am Tag bestellen.
- eBusiness – die Revolution hat begonnen!
- Besuchen Sie uns dieses Jahr an einem unserer Stände auf der Messe in Hannover.

Mediation: Textwiedergabe in deutscher Sprache

AUFGABE 1

Ihr Unternehmen ist seit langem auf dem englischen Markt tätig. Nächste Woche findet das Quartalstreffen statt. Ihre Chefin ist bis dahin noch auf einer wichtigen Geschäftsreise und bittet Sie, nachfolgenden Text ins Deutsche zu übertragen. Verwenden Sie dazu die Vorlage auf Seite 107.

SURVEY SHOWS WELCOME IMPROVEMENT BUT RECOVERY STILL FRAGILE

The slight improvement in the UK's economy must be carefully supported to avoid further rises in unemployment and an end to export growth, the British Chambers of Commerce (BCC) warned today. The BCC survey shows that the manufacturing sector recorded increases in Q1 (first quarter) for home sales and orders, export sales and orders, and plant and machinery investment.

The domestic market
The manufacturing sector improved further in Q1, but the results are still relatively weak.

Export market
The manufacturing sector's export performance improved markedly in Q1.

Investment
The balance of manufacturing firms planning to increase investment in plant and machinery rose 7 points in Q1 to +15 %, highest for two years. Intentions to invest in training remained unchanged, at +18 %.

Survey size
The British Chambers of Commerce Quarterly Economic Survey covers almost 5,000 companies employing 300,000 people. The respondents are spread throughout the United Kingdom. Companies were surveyed by postal questionnaire over the period from 27 February to 20 March.

Survey composition
In the manufacturing sector, 1,328 firms employing 114,518 people responded. 589 (44 %) of manufacturing respondents are exporters.

Quelle: BCC British Chambers of Commerce

Entwicklung der verarbeitenden Industrie – Umfrage der BCC, 1. Quartal

1. Allgemeines

_____

_____

_____

_____

_____

_____

2. Konkrete Zahlen für den Fertigungssektor
   a. Inland:

_____

_____

_____

   b. Export:

_____

_____

   c. Investitionen:

_____

_____

_____

_____

3. Details zur Durchführung der Umfrage
   a. Umfang:

_____

_____

_____

_____

   b. Zusammensetzung:

_____

_____

_____

_____

AUFGABE 2

Sie arbeiten in der Einkaufsabteilung eines Handelsbetriebes. Auf der Suche nach neuen Lieferanten stoßen Sie im Internet auf einen interessanten Anbieter aus den USA. Ihre Gruppenleiterin bittet Sie, die Zahlungsbedingungen zur besseren Vergleichbarkeit ins Deutsche zu übertragen.

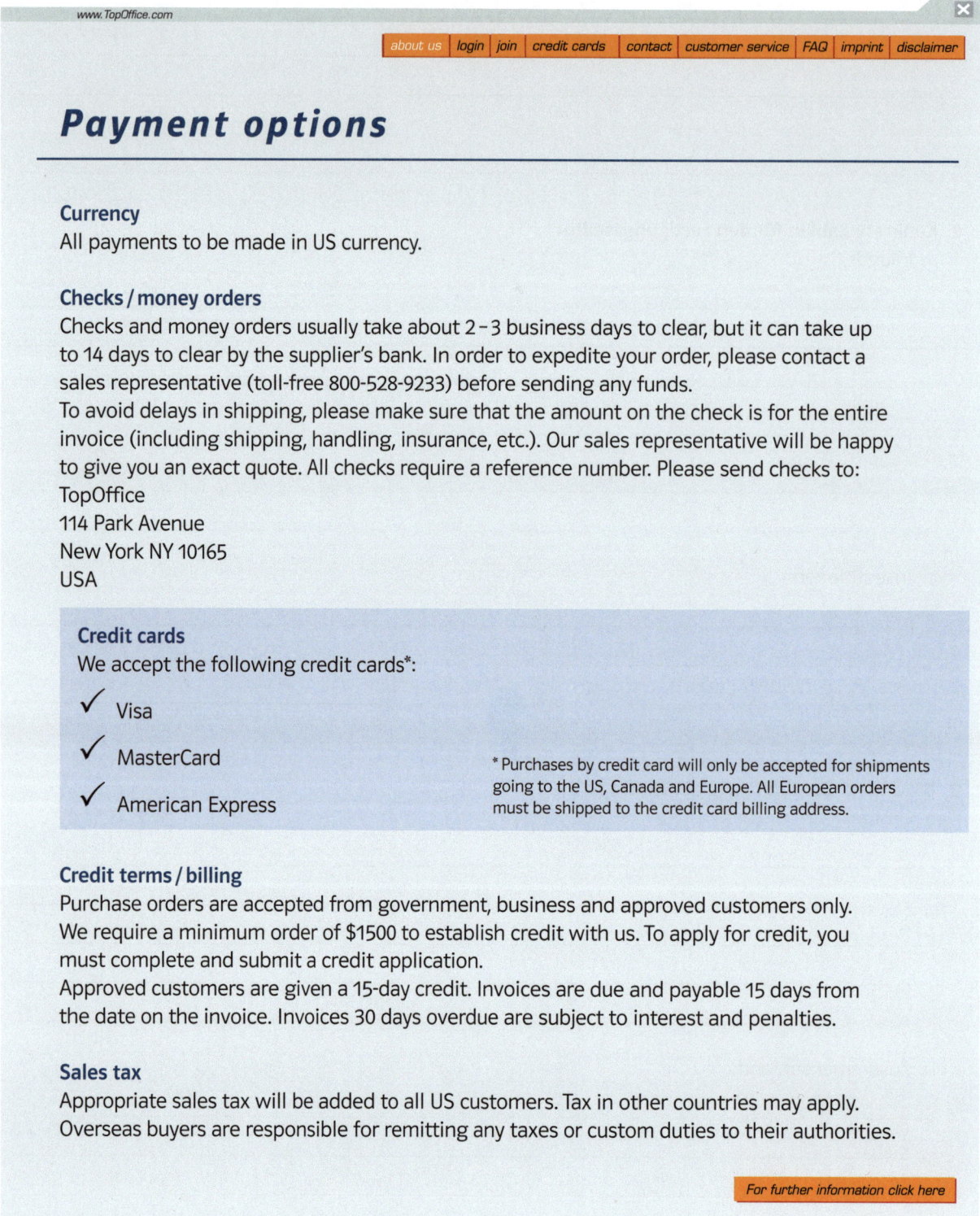

www.TopOffice.com

about us | login | join | credit cards | contact | customer service | FAQ | imprint | disclaimer

Payment options

Currency
All payments to be made in US currency.

Checks / money orders
Checks and money orders usually take about 2–3 business days to clear, but it can take up to 14 days to clear by the supplier's bank. In order to expedite your order, please contact a sales representative (toll-free 800-528-9233) before sending any funds.
To avoid delays in shipping, please make sure that the amount on the check is for the entire invoice (including shipping, handling, insurance, etc.). Our sales representative will be happy to give you an exact quote. All checks require a reference number. Please send checks to:
TopOffice
114 Park Avenue
New York NY 10165
USA

Credit cards
We accept the following credit cards*:

✓ Visa

✓ MasterCard

✓ American Express

* Purchases by credit card will only be accepted for shipments going to the US, Canada and Europe. All European orders must be shipped to the credit card billing address.

Credit terms / billing
Purchase orders are accepted from government, business and approved customers only. We require a minimum order of $1500 to establish credit with us. To apply for credit, you must complete and submit a credit application.
Approved customers are given a 15-day credit. Invoices are due and payable 15 days from the date on the invoice. Invoices 30 days overdue are subject to interest and penalties.

Sales tax
Appropriate sales tax will be added to all US customers. Tax in other countries may apply. Overseas buyers are responsible for remitting any taxes or custom duties to their authorities.

For further information click here

---

to expedite – beschleunigen; penalty – Mahngebühr; to remit – überweisen, weiterleiten

AUFGABE 3

Ihr Ausbilder bittet Sie folgenden Text über Leasing in den USA ins Deutsche zu übertragen.

Why do businesses choose leasing?

Cash flow is a major concern for most companies, especially small businesses. Because buying new or used equipment can be one of the largest expenses a company faces, many businesses need a solution that allows them to get what they need without diminishing their cash flow.

Leasing offers numerous advantages over other types of financing, including tax deductions, balance sheet management, immediate write-offs, great flexibility, customized solutions, better asset management, flexible end-of-term options, easy upgrades, and fast processing.

Research shows that eight out of ten US companies choose to lease some or all of their equipment. This year alone, more than $208 billion in equipment will be leased in the United States.

AUFGABE 4

Ihr Ausbildungsunternehmen ist sich nicht sicher, ob die Musik, die ein Kollege für das Mitarbeiterfest aus dem Internet heruntergeladen hat, legal einsetzbar ist. Ihre Vorgesetzte bittet Sie deshalb den folgenden Text ins Deutsche zu übersetzen.

Digital piracy rife

A new survey found three quarters of those asked said they'd downloaded tracks without paying. And many are confused about what's legal and what isn't.

Despite a hardline record industry campaign to stamp out digital piracy, the figures show just one in six said they exclusively use paid-for services to buy music on the internet.

But Matt Philips from the British Phonographic Industry maintains progress is being made:
"Download services would be far more popular if we gave all the music away for free," he said. "But of course we wouldn't have a business then – it's important that you charge for the product and that money can be re-invested in discovering new talent."

The survey, conducted by Mori for AOL UK, also found confusion amongst consumers over whether they were breaking copyright laws by using illegal sites. Only four in ten said that they understood the law.

The British Phonographic Industry had a hardline campaigning against those who illegally share music over the web. It's taken legal action against more than 150 internet users, half of them paid settlements of up to £6,500 to avoid court action.

Quelle: BBC Music News

AUFGABE 5

Ihr Unternehmen ist bereits international tätig und bietet eine spezielle Dienstleistung im Bereich Marketing an. Nun möchten Sie auch am britischen Markt expandieren. Ihr Chef beauftragt Sie, die Kosten für die Eintragung eines Warenzeichens herauszufinden. Sie finden im Internet eine entsprechende Seite mit FAQs und übersetzen diese für ihn.

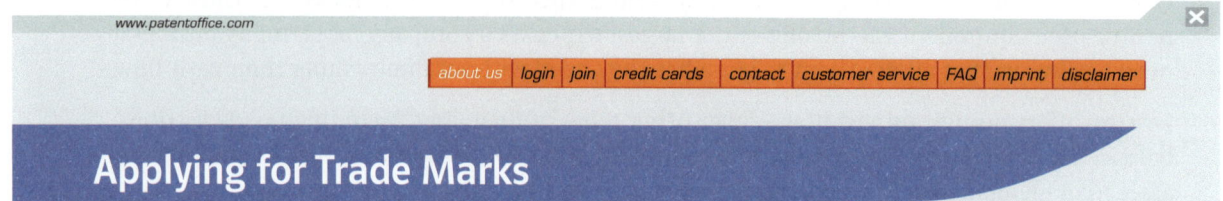

www.patentoffice.com

about us | login | join | credit cards | contact | customer service | FAQ | imprint | disclaimer

Applying for Trade Marks

Frequently Asked Questions

1 How much does it cost to apply for a trade mark?

The fee for an application is £ (pounds sterling) 200. This includes one class of goods or services. For every other class you apply for, it costs a further £ (pounds sterling) 50 for each class.

2 Can I get a refund if my application is turned down?

No. The application fee covers the cost of us processing and examining your application.

3 Can I get a world-wide trade mark registration?

This is currently not possible, but as well as applying to register your trade mark in the UK, you may also:

(1) apply for a European Community Trade Mark (CTM)

(2) apply, via the UK Patent Office, to register your trade mark through the international "Madrid Protocol" system which covers various countries around the world which have joined the Protocol

4 How long does my trade mark registration last?

Your registration lasts ten years from the date of registration. We will write to you a few months before the renewal date, asking if you wish to renew your trade mark for a further ten years.

5 If I get a registration, can I sell it?

Yes. A trade mark is legally described as "intellectual property" and so you can sell it if you want. However, if you wish to do this, we recommend that you get legal advice from an attorney who can advise you on the correct procedure.

6 Do I have to pay costs if someone opposes my mark?

If someone opposes your mark and you withdraw it or lose your challenge to an opposition, you may have to pay towards the other person's costs.

Quelle: The Patent Office

AUFGABE 6

Ihr Unternehmen benötigt für die Neueröffnung einer Geschäftsstelle in Großbritannien ein Geschäfts-konto. Bei einer Online-Recherche entdecken Sie folgende Informationen. Übertragen Sie diese für Ihren Chef ins Deutsche.

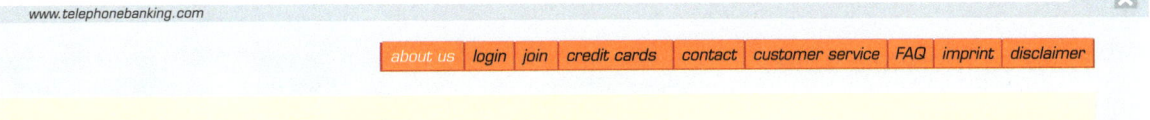

www.telephonebanking.com

| about us | login | join | credit cards | contact | customer service | FAQ | imprint | disclaimer |

Telephone banking

With business telephone banking, you can do your banking from home and from your office. You can carry out a range of transactions and access a number of services.

Benefits

✓ UK-based call centres – our advisers understand your needs
✓ No extra costs – there are no charges for telephone banking; all you pay for is the call
✓ Round-the-clock access – every day of the year (System updates will mean that some services are unavailable for short periods in the early hours of the morning.)
✓ Personal accounts management – deal with all your business and personal finances
✓ Employee access – your authorised employees can be given information-only access to allow them to check account balances

Features

✓ Transfer money – immediate transfer of funds to another account
✓ Pay bills – pay your suppliers, staff or general business expenditures
✓ Manage payments – set up, change and cancel standing orders and direct debits
✓ Check your balance – order a statement and check your recent transactions
✓ Order foreign currency – to be delivered to your business or collected from any branch
✓ Order a cheque book – or a pay-in book or a banker's draft

AUFGABE 7

Ihr Vorgesetzter hat von einer Geschäftsreise nach London den Flyer eines Unternehmens mitgebracht, das sich auf Wirtschaftsauskünfte spezialisiert hat. Er bittet Sie, für eine Abteilungsbesprechung die wichtigsten Punkte zusammenzufassen.

Business Guard

Are customers creditworthy?

It is essential to know how creditworthy your business customers and suppliers are so that you can avoid the risk of late payment or bad debt. In uncertain economic times, Business Guard will give your business access to vital credit-related information on (potential) customers and suppliers:

– Access credit checks, reports and information on business customers in the UK.
– Be alerted to key changes that can affect a customer's credit risk.
– Protect your supply chain and avoid losses through corporate fraud and ID theft.

– Access data on approximately 2.8 million limited companies, 4.8 million company directors and 3.4 million non-limited businesses in the UK.

Choose from our two Business Guard packages to suit your needs. Standard offers an economical pay-as-you-go service, while Star offers a more inclusive low-cost monthly subscription service:

– Standard: Access as many credit reports and alerts as your business requires. There is an annual fee of £30 with each report costing £8.50.
– Star: Access unlimited credit reports and alerts on up to 20 nominated companies. There is an annual fee of £180 payable at £15 per month.

AUFGABE 8

Die Marketing Abteilung Ihres Unternehmens hat von einer Außendienstmitarbeiterin einen englischen Leitfaden über Verkaufsförderung bekommen. Sie bittet Sie, in einer Dokumentation für die künftigen Auszubildenden die wichtigsten Punkte auf Deutsch zusammenzufassen.

How to increase sales

General aspects

Appearance of the customer

First and foremost, appearances do not make your customer. Although a woman who is dressed in brand-name clothing or wearing expensive jewelry may have money, this does not mean that a woman who lacks these things cannot afford the products in your store.

Appearance of the shop assistant

Appearances on your part however, are extremely important to your volume of sales. Be sure to dress professionally and, if at all possible, try to wear or model the items you are selling.

Know your products

Be sure that you are familiar with all the products you are selling, because this will mean that you are able to answer any questions. Customers will have a pleasing shopping experience, which may lead to them coming back to buy more of your products.

Aspects regarding female customers

Are your customers mainly women? Do you find it harder to sell your products to women? Well, here are some general rules you should follow to become more successful:

1. Employ women in your company – on the sales floor and even in repairs. A male repair person may put a woman in an intimidating situation, especially elderly women. Female staff give your female clientele somebody to relate to. Women are more likely to buy from somebody they feel understands their wishes and needs, rather than from someone who they feel doesn't.

2. Hold a Buy One Get One Free Sale or a Bring A Friend Day, or invite female customers to an Exclusive Champagne Fashion Show in order to promote the sale of your products.

AUFGABE 1

Rezeption: Hörverstehen

20 Punkte

A Maria Schmitt macht bei Home Entertainment Ltd. in Weymouth / UK ein Praktikum. Hören Sie dem Gespräch mit Gareth Henderson von Home Entertainment Ltd. zu und beantworten Sie folgende Fragen. Hören Sie sich das Gespräch zweimal an.

1. Seit wann arbeitet Maria in der neuen Abteilung?

    _____

2. In welcher Abteilung hat sie vorher gearbeitet?

    _____

3. Die Incoterms werden bei Home Entertainment verwendet bei:
    ☐ allen Verträgen.
    ☐ allen inländischen Verträgen.
    ☐ allen internationalen Verträgen.

4. Ergänzen Sie die Angaben zu dem Auftrag über HE 200 Portable Laptop Speakers.

    a. Verkaufte Stückzahl: _____

    b. Welche Incoterms wurden für die HE 200 Portable Laptop Speakers vereinbart?
    ☐ CIF
    ☐ ex works
    ☐ FOB

    c. Wer ist hier für die Verladung auf LKWs verantwortlich?
    ☐ Verkäufer
    ☐ Käufer

5. Ergänzen Sie die Angaben zu dem Auftrag über Portable Bluetooth Speakers.

    a. Verkaufte Stückzahl: _____

    b. Welche Incoterms wurden für die Portable Bluetooth Speakers vertraglich vereinbart?
    ☐ CIF
    ☐ ex works
    ☐ FOB

6. Welche Aussage zu den Incoterms ist richtig?
    ☐ Sie gelten bei allen internationalen Verträgen automatisch als vereinbart.
    ☐ Sie gelten nur, wenn sie schriftlich vereinbart wurden.
    ☐ Sie stellen internationales Recht dar und gelten immer.

7. In welcher Stadt wurden die Incoterms entwickelt? _____

8. Wann wurden die Incoterms entwickelt? _____

9. Wie viele Incoterms gibt es? _____

10. In wie vielen Sprachen gibt es die Incoterms? _____

11. Wofür steht die Abkürzung ICC?
    ☐ International Commercial Chamber
    ☐ Internal Chamber of Commerce
    ☐ International Chamber of Commerce

B Sie hören den Anrufbeantworter an Ihrem Arbeitsplatz ab, auf dem eine Nachricht hinterlassen wurde. Tragen Sie die Angaben in die entsprechenden Kästchen ein. Hören Sie sich die Nachricht zweimal an.

Name
Order no.
Phone no.

AUFGABE 2

Rezeption: Leseverstehen   20 Punkte

Lesen Sie folgenden Text und beantworten Sie die Fragen auf Seite 115.

Loyalty cards

A loyalty card program allows a retail business to collect data about its customers. Customers are offered product discounts, coupons or bonus points in exchange for their participation in the program. Often they get special offers that are not available to non-participating customers.

Loyalty cards mostly look like plastic credit cards and have a barcode or magnetic strip that is scanned at the point of sale (POS). The card identifies the customer and sends information on what the customer bought to a database.

The main result of a recent study carried out by an advertising agency was that consumers who take part in customer loyalty programs generally spend more money than non-members. The study was conducted over a six-month time span and across 11 retail categories including home improvement, electronics, grocery stores and book stores.

To see what kind of people use loyalty cards, the study looked primarily at the following categories: gender, age, marital status, children under the age of 18 in the family, and income.

An interesting finding was that 62 percent of the women interviewed used loyalty cards, but only 54 percent of the men. It is important to know who is likely to join a loyalty program so that stores can adjust their product range and customer service to reach their most loyal customers.

What kinds of people take part in loyalty card programs in the different retail categories? According to the survey, members tend to have one or more of the following characteristics (by retail category):
– Home improvement and DIY shops: men, married, with children under the age of 18
– Electronics: men, under 65 years of age
– Drug stores: women, living in big cities
– Discount supermarkets: women, married, with children under the age of 18
– Book stores: women, with an income of more than $30,000 per year.

Which is the most popular loyalty program nationwide? Not surprisingly, the grocery store programs are most popular. In this study, over 77 percent of those interviewed were members of grocery store loyalty programs.

1. Warum sind Kundenkarten wichtig für den Einzelhandel? (1 P.)

_____

_____

2. Welche Angebote/Vorteile erhält der Kunde mit einer Kundenkarte? Nennen Sie vier. (4 P.)

_____

_____

3. Welche beiden Systeme zum Speichern bzw. Lesen von Daten auf den Kundenkarten gibt es? (2 P.)

_____

_____

4. Von wem wurde die Studie durchgeführt? (1 P.)

_____

5. Welches Hauptergebnis ergibt sich aus der Studie? (1 P.)

_____

_____

6. Über welchen Zeitraum wurde die Studie erhoben? (1 P.)

_____

7. Welchen Umfang hatte die Studie? (1 P.)

_____

8. Nennen Sie drei Kriterien, die in der Studie untersucht wurden. (3 P.)

_____

_____

_____

9. Warum ist es für den Einzelhandel wichtig, die Kundenpräferenzen genau zu kennen?
   Nennen Sie einen Grund. (1 P.)

_____

_____

10. Welche Merkmale haben die Inhaber von Kundenkarten typischerweise in folgenden Branchen?
    (4 P.)

    a. Elektronikmärkte: _____

    _____

    b. Buchhandel: _____

    _____

11. Welche Kundenkarten sind bei den Verbrauchern am beliebtesten? (1 P.)

_____

AUFGABE 3

Produktion	30 Punkte

Sie arbeiten bei der Firma Magma GmbH, die Werbeartikel aller Art vertreibt. Sie werden gebeten anhand des folgenden Memos aus dem Wareneingang und einer Notiz von Ihrem Vorgesetzten einen Brief an die Lieferfirma United Presents Ltd. in Shanghai zu schreiben. Erstellen Sie bitte den Brieftext einschließlich Anrede und Schlussformel.

MAGMA GmbH
Gesprächsnotiz

Verfasst von: Thomas Berg (Wareneingang)

Am: 15.05.201_

Betrifft: Bestellnr. RV / 271 / 03 vom 30. April dieses Jahres

Beanstandungen:
- von den 1.000 bestellten Flaschenöffnern wurden nur 500 geliefert
- die 200 gelieferten USB-Sticks haben anstelle der bestellten 4 GB Speichervolumen nur 2 GB Speichervolumen

- Bitte für pünktliche Lieferung bedanken
- Vorschlag an Lieferanten: sofortige Lieferung der fehlenden Flaschenöffner
- Preisnachlass von 50 % für 2 GB USB-Sticks, da Kunde sie dringend benötigt

AUFGABE 4

Mediation	30 Punkte

Sie arbeiten in einem Personaldienstleistungsunternehmen. Da Ihr Unternehmen auch englisch-sprachige Fachkräfte für einen Großauftrag sucht, erhalten Sie die Aufgabe, folgenden Bewerber-leitfaden ins Englische zu übertragen.

Wie bewirbt man sich erfolgreich?

- Schreiben Sie Ihre Bewerbung immer mit dem PC – handschriftliche Lebensläufe sind nicht mehr zeitgemäß.
- Verwenden Sie Papier einer guten Qualität und vermeiden Sie farbiges Papier.
- Gliedern Sie Ihren Lebenslauf nach **persönlichen Daten**, **Ausbildung** und **Beruf** und verzichten Sie auf die Auflistung von alltäglichen Hobbys.
- Geben Sie mindestens zwei vertrauenswürdige Personen als Referenz an. Überlegen Sie genau wer hierfür als geeignet erscheint.
- Achten Sie darauf, dass keine Lücken im Lebenslauf sind, d. h. Sie sollten keine Zeitspanne unerklärter Beschäftigungslosigkeit haben.
- Verwenden Sie ein neueres Foto, das von einem Fotografen eigens dafür aufgenommen wurde.
- Kleben Sie das Foto auf das Deckblatt Ihrer Bewerbung.
- Stellen Sie sicher, dass Sie alle aufgeführten Anlagen auch wirklich komplett mitschicken.
- Und noch ein Tipp: Haben Sie Geduld – ein bis zwei Wochen Wartezeit für eine Rückantwort gelten als normal.

AUFGABE 1 ⊚ A3.27

Rezeption: Hörverstehen   **20 Punkte**

Ihr Unternehmen möchte seine Messepräsenz verstärken. Ihr Chef bittet Sie daher, das folgende Interview anzuhören und die Informationen zur GlobalTech für ihn zusammenzustellen.

GlobalTech

1. Wann und wo wird die Ausstellung stattfinden?

   _____

   _____

2. Welche namhaften Firmen haben bereits zugesagt?

   _____

   _____

3. Welche Schwerpunkte hat die GlobalTech in diesem Jahr?

   _____

   _____

   _____

4. Warum findet die Ausstellung an drei Veranstaltungsorten gleichzeitig statt?

   _____

   _____

   _____

5. Wo können Aussteller weitere Informationen über die GlobalTech erhalten?

   _____

   _____

6. Welche Kosten entstehen für die Aussteller für
   a. einen Ausstellungsort?

   _____

   b. alle drei Ausstellungsorte?

   _____

7. Was beinhaltet das Ausstellungspaket?

   _____

   _____

   _____

   _____

   _____

AUFGABE 2

Rezeption: Leseverstehen   **20 Punkte**

Ihr Unternehmen ist auf Standortsuche in Großbritannien. Neben anderen Standorten ist Manchester im Gespräch. Beantworten Sie anhand des Textes die Fragen auf Seite 119 auf Deutsch.

Business Performance Plan

The Business Performance Plan allows the Council to measure its performance for services to businesses. This plan monitors performance, sets targets and details our priorities for the coming year.

Manchester has good reason to be proud of its thriving business community. The 17,000 companies based here are central to the Manchester economy and help to make it the kind of city where people choose to live, work and play.

Our city continues to build its reputation as a prime European business location and the Council is committed to making it an even better place to do business. We pledged action to fight crime and anti-social behaviour, to look at transport problems and to improve the appearance of your local environment, and have been working steadily with our partners to fulfil that promise. We are making clear progress – but still have a lot more to do.

The facts

Of the 17,000 businesses that call Manchester home, 88 % are small companies with a workforce of less than 25. The number of people employed in the city rose by 2.12 % to 289,000 and over 2,000 new jobs were created in Wythenshawe, Cheetham, Moss Side, East Manchester and along the Stockport Road Corridor.

More satisfied customers

Every year we ask local businesses what they think of the way we deliver our services in their area. Our latest Business Survey, a telephone survey of a representative sample of 306 Manchester companies, shows 70 % to be "fairly" or "very" satisfied with our performance – quite an increase on the 36 % who gave us their approval the previous year!

We're on the road to better public transport

Last year we worked closely with the Greater Manchester Passenger Transport Authority to make further improvements to Manchester's public transport system and were applauded for our successful strategy to make sure the high volume of traffic passing through the city during the Commonwealth Games caused the minimum disruption to normal city life.

With the Government's go-ahead for Metrolink extension finally in place, new lines through North Manchester to Oldham and Rochdale; East Manchester to Ashton and South Manchester; and Wythenshawe to Manchester Airport will be operating in the near future.

Just the ticket for parking

47 % of businesses believe car parking in Manchester has improved, against 33 % last year. There are 52 car parks now providing high quality parking facilities many with state of the art CCTV protection for people working in and visiting the city centre.

Cleaning up

Environmental 'hit squads' are set to clean up the business environment, clearing rubbish and cleaning graffiti. To shed further light on the issue, we'll be making significant improvements to street lighting across the city.

This year we want to see the number of business people satisfied with litter and refuse removal rise from 46% to 56% and environmental services generally from 57% to 67%. We know from our survey that 53% of businesses believe their environment to be acceptably clean, and 56% of you are satisfied with the physical condition of Manchester roads.

Safer for business

32% of respondents to our business survey believe that crime is falling. Our efforts to make Manchester a safer place to do business continue with a Business Crime Action Plan that targets crime hotspots and offers security advice to businesses. The Action Plan will be supported by a website that will also encourage people to report criminal activity that affects their business. Small retailers in Woodhouse Park and Moston can operate more safely thanks to our work to make premises more secure and to deter local crime and disorder. Incidents of youth nuisance are down and an alcohol ban in the areas around shopping parades is paying dividends.

What do you think?

To make Manchester a better place to do business we need to know what you the business community think about the city and the services we deliver.

We'd like to know what you consider to be the three main issues affecting business in Manchester.

Quelle: Manchester City Council

1. Wozu dient der Business Performance Plan (BPP) der Stadt Manchester im Einzelnen? (3 P.)

   _____

   _____

2. Nennen Sie drei Ziele, die die Stadt Manchester mit dem BPP verfolgt. (3 P.)

   _____

   _____

3. Um welche Art von Unternehmen handelt es sich in der Mehrzahl in Manchester in Bezug auf Größe und Mitarbeiterzahl? (2 P.)

   _____

   _____

4. In welchen Abständen führt die Stadt Manchester die Umfrage durch? (1 P.)

   _____

5. Beschreiben Sie Art und Umfang der letzten Umfrage. (2 P.)

   _____

6. Wie viel Prozent der Befragten war mit den kommunalen Dienstleistungen ziemlich oder sehr zufrieden? (1 P.)

   _____

7. Wie sind die Parkplätze überwiegend ausgestattet? (1 P.)

   _____

8. Eine Maßnahme zur Verbesserung der Sauberkeit der Stadt war die Schaffung von so genannten „Umwelteinsatzgruppen".
   a. Welche Aufgaben erfüllen sie? (2 P.)

   _____

   b. Welche weitere Maßnahme ist geplant? (1 P.)

   _____

9. Ein weiteres Ziel ist die Senkung der Kriminalitätsrate.
   a. Welches Ergebnis zeigt die Studie in diesem Zusammenhang? (1 P.)

   _____

   b. Welche Angebote werden den Geschäftsleuten gemacht? (2 P.)

   _____

   _____

   c. Welche Erfolge konnten bereits erzielt werden? (2 P.)

   _____

   _____

AUFGABE 3

Produktion   **30 Punkte**

Ihr Unternehmen veranstaltet jedes Jahr ein Treffen, bei dem die Verkaufsrepräsentanten aus ganz Europa zusammenkommen. Dieses Jahr ist der Veranstaltungsort Bristol. Sie haben bereits mit einer Mitarbeiterin des Bristol Conference Centre (53 Queen Square, Bristol, BS1 4LH) telefoniert und einige Fragen vorab geklärt. Schreiben Sie nun einen inhaltlich und formal korrekten Brief an Monica Hawkins, in dem Sie Ihre Wünsche konkretisieren. Folgende Stichpunkte sollten enthalten sein:

- Nehmen Sie Bezug auf das Telefongespräch von heute morgen.
- Bitten Sie um Reservierung der Festival Hall des Bristol Conference Centre von 10. bis 12. September dieses Jahres.
- Veranstaltungsdauer ist jeweils von 9 Uhr bis 19 Uhr.
- Während der Pausen (um 10.30 Uhr und um 16 Uhr) sollen Getränke und kleine Snacks serviert werden.
- Bitten Sie um die Buchung von Hotelzimmern im Bristol Conference Hotel (56 Einzelzimmer und 8 Doppelzimmer).
- Mittagessen (ca. 13 Uhr) soll ebenfalls im Bristol Conference Hotel stattfinden.
- Bitten Sie um Zusendung von Informationsmaterial (Speisekarte, Hotelbroschüre, Stadtplan, Veranstaltungskalender von Bristol) und um eine Bestätigung inklusive Kostenaufstellung.

AUFGABE 4

Mediation   **30 Punkte**

Ihr Unternehmen möchte seine guten Kontakte nach England in Zukunft noch verbessern und denkt darüber nach eine Mitgliedschaft bei der Londoner IHK zu beantragen. Ihr Chef bittet Sie nun den folgenden Text für ein Gespräch aufzubereiten. Übertragen Sie ihn sinngemäß ins Deutsche und achten Sie auf eine übersichtliche Form.

Overseas Membership

Overseas membership of London Chamber of Commerce and Industry costs £150 + VAT per annum and offers companies based outside the UK who do not have a UK registered office the opportunity to be part of the UK's biggest business organisation.

Becoming an overseas member of the London Chamber gives you:

- Access to the Members' Only Zone on the London Chamber website – your user name and password will be sent to you on registration

- A listing on the online searchable Members' Directory to enable you to promote your business – this also provides you with the ability to search for other members

- An entry in the London Chamber Annual Members' Directory in the Overseas Members category

- Access to the Members' Lounge at 33 Queen Street when visiting the UK

- Discounts of 10 % on venue hire at London Chamber

- Attendance at London Chamber events at member rate when visiting the UK – visit the online events diary to keep up to date with what is happening

- A copy of the London Chamber monthly e-newsletter – this member-only publication includes business news, business tips, updates on Chamber events, campaigns and services.

Quelle: London Chamber of Commerce and Industry

AUFGABE 1   ◉ A3.28

Rezeption: Hörverstehen	20 Punkte

Auf einer Messe hören Sie ein Interview von Frank Miller mit Anna Jones, der Geschäftsführerin der amerikanischen Firma Fun Foods Inc., die ausschließlich Produkte aus biologischem Anbau vertreibt. Hören Sie sich den Text zweimal an und beantworten Sie folgende Fragen auf Deutsch.

1. Wie hat sich der biologische Anbau in den letzten Jahren entwickelt? (1 P.)

   _____

2. Wie sehen die Zukunftserwartungen aus? (1 P.)

   _____

3. Welche Probleme haben sich aus dem schnellen Wachstum ergeben? (2 P.)

   _____

4. Ergänzen Sie die Zahlen zu folgenden Angaben. (3 P.)

   a. Fläche für biologischen Anbau in den USA:

   neueste Zahlen: _____ Zahlen des Vorjahres: _____

   b. Umsatz an Bioprodukten in den USA im vergangenen Jahr: _____

5. Erstellen Sie eine Rangliste der US-Bundesstaaten hinsichtlich des Absatzes von Bioprodukten. (3 P.)

Kalifornien	Texas
Oregon	Washington
Pennsylvania	Wisconsin

6. Ergänzen Sie die Prozentzahlen für die Absatzmärkte. (2 P.)

   a. Absatz im Umkreis von unter 100 Meilen: _____

   b. Absatz im Umkreis von 100 bis 500 Meilen: _____

7. Welche weiteren Ergebnisse brachte die Studie hervor? Kreuzen Sie die genannten Ergebnisse an. (3 P.)

   ☐ Der Anteil von Bioprodukten an Nahrungsmittelverkäufen insgesamt ist auf 3,7 % gestiegen.

   ☐ Die Kosten für die biologische Produktion sind explodiert.

   ☐ Die Mehrzahl der Käufe von Bioprodukten erfolgte in Supermarktketten.

   ☐ Die Nachfrage nach Bioprodukten ist in der Altersgruppe der 30-45 Jährigen am höchsten.

   ☐ Durch den Einsatz von biologischen Düngemitteln konnte der Ertrag gesteigert werden.

   ☐ Obst und Gemüse machen den größten Anteil aus.

8. Worauf ist der vergleichsweise geringe Anstieg in Großbritannien zurückzuführen? (1 P.)

   _____

9. In welchen weiteren Branchen stieg der Umsatz von Bioprodukten? (3 P.)

   _____

10. In welchem europäischen Land werden die meisten Bioprodukte verkauft? (1 P.)

   _____

AUFGABE 2

Rezeption: Leseverstehen **20 Punkte**

Ihr Unternehmen überlegt, fair gehandelten Kaffee aus Afrika ins Verkaufsprogramm aufzunehmen.
Lesen Sie folgenden Text und bearbeiten Sie anschließend die Fragen auf Seite 124.

Smell the coffee

It's one of the strange things that in a country where vast quantities of coffee is grown very few local people will ever taste it. There's no tradition of coffee drinking – certainly not comparable with the appetite in the Western world. But maybe that doesn't matter because the smell of coffee is certainly in the air in other ways.

Small scale farmers are getting together to form fair trade co-operatives. This means that by working together, pooling resources, sharing expertise on quality while joining forces with European producers they can radically change the outlook of their families and villages.

The village of Kizi might appear to be similar to many African communities. People work hard in the fields, herding animals, carrying produce to and from market on their heads while children run around in often threadbare clothes.

But beneath the surface there is a huge transformation taking place. The co-operative has built a school and is employing teachers. Youngsters as young as four are starting to become fluent not only in their own local language but in French and English, too. Something they only too readily demonstrate to visitors. Soon they will have a solid grounding in a range of subjects which their parents hope will eventually give them a future they couldn't have hoped for them before fair trade came to Kizi.

Back in the village a string of small huts have become hairdressers. A young man with the help of a recently purchased generator shows off his new clippers and offers a haircut to any passers-by brave enough to take the chair. A little further down more huts sell cooked food. Alongside them stands an African pub. The drinkers have little in the way of furniture and alcohol only comes out of bottles.

But all of this is much bigger than it seems at first sight. It's a certain sign of hope. A place where – for some – there is finally additional income which is kick-starting business and bringing prosperity. There's even a bank where small loans can be made by the co-operative to help people get new businesses started.

Most people in the village are still working in the fields growing coffee. But by working with registered Fairtrade companies they are promised a much better return for themselves and the community. They are promised a premium on their coffee beans. Some of this extra money they will receive as individuals for whatever they wish to buy. The co-operative also gets a payment. Recently they bought a lorry so collecting the coffee from small and isolated farms is easier. They can also take their coffee to newly built washing plants where careful processing has made their coffee among the finest in the world.

There's also much pride in Kizi. One of their farmers Jemima has been chosen by a Fairtrade coffee producer to use her face on their products. She has become the object of interest for film crews and journalists wanting to tell this remarkable story of how farming is changing lives in Africa. Jemima can increasingly find herself standing in the village in front of cameras holding a pack of the coffee which can now be found in some UK supermarkets.

More and more coffee farmers are wanting to taste the benefits of producing beans under the Fairtrade banner. They know the UK market for Fairtrade products has doubled this year alone.

Rwandan farmers may not be drinking the coffee but they are certainly smelling the wind of change.

Quelle: BBC NEWS

1. Was ist die besondere Situation in Bezug auf Kaffee in Ruanda? (2 P.)

   _____

   _____

2. Welche Vorteile ergeben sich für Farmer aus der Zusammenarbeit in Fairtrade Kooperativen. (3 P.)

   _____

   _____

   _____

3. Wie profitieren die Kinder des Dorfes von der Kooperative? (4 P.)

   _____

   _____

   _____

4. Welche weiteren Geschäfte sind inzwischen im Dorf zu finden? (3 P.)

   _____

   _____

5. Welche positiven Auswirkungen hat das zusätzliche Einkommen, das im Dorf erworben wird? (2 P.)

   _____

   _____

6. Was verspricht Fairtrade den Farmern, die sich registrieren lassen? (2 P.)

   _____

   _____

7. Wozu dient der LKW, der kürzlich angeschafft werden konnte? (2 P.)

   _____

   _____

8. Wie ist die künftige Akzeptanz von Fairtrade seitens der Farmer einzuschätzen? (1 P.)

   _____

9. Wie hat sich der Verkauf von Fairtrade Kaffee auf dem britischen Markt entwickelt? (1 P.)

   _____

AUFGABE 3

Produktion   **30 Punkte**

Sie arbeiten gerade in der Abteilung Events Management eines großen international tätigen Unternehmens, das jährlich im Rahmen einer Veranstaltung, die Geschäftspartner des Jahres auszeichnet. Formulieren Sie die Einladung an die Firma Pure Excellence plc (15 Windmill Street, Manchester, M2 3GX) zu Händen Patricia Roberts. Schreiben Sie einen inhaltlich und formal korrekten Brief mit folgendem Inhalt:

- Sie freuen sich sehr mitzuteilen, dass das Unternehmen Pure Excellence zum Geschäftspartner des Jahres gewählt wurde und laden zu der Veranstaltung „Business Partner of the Year" ein.
- Termin: 24. Juli dieses Jahres, 19 Uhr
- Ort: CCC (Congress and Conference Center) in Nürnberg
- Ablauf:
  - Begrüßung und Ansprache des Vorsitzenden
  - Vortrag über die neuesten Entwicklungen und Zukunftsperspektiven der Branche
  - Preisverleihung
  - Buffet
- Repräsentanten der Preisträgerfirma werden als Gäste Ihres Unternehmens in dem 5-Sterne-Hotel Nürnberger Hof untergebracht.
- Bitten Sie um baldige Bestätigung der Teilnahme mit Angabe der Anzahl der teilnehmenden Personen.
- Weisen Sie darauf hin, dass die Veranstaltung auch die Möglichkeit zu Gesprächen und zur Anbahnung von neuen Geschäftsbeziehungen bietet.
- Formulieren Sie einen höflichen Schlusssatz.

AUFGABE 4

Mediation   **30 Punkte**

Ihre Firma hat eine Auszeichnung für besonders soziales und umweltbewusstes Verhalten erhalten. Bei einer Veranstaltung mit Geschäftspartnern möchte Ihre Chefin die Besonderheiten Ihres Unternehmens vorstellen und in diesem Zusammenhang auch für die Fair Trade-Sache werben. Ihre Chefin bittet Sie deshalb, folgenden Text für ein Informationsblatt ins Deutsche zu übertragen.

Fairtrade Facts

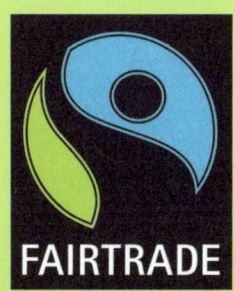

Fairtrade is about better prices, decent working conditions, local sustainability and fair terms of trade for farmers and workers in the developing world. Fairtrade is an alternative approach to conventional international trade.
If a product is part of the Fairtrade system, farmers are:
- Paid a guaranteed minimum price that covers costs and exceeds the world market price
- Given a premium to invest in their local community
- Guaranteed long-term and more direct trading relations
- Helped to improve their working conditions and their environment
- Members of democratic organisations, usually a co-operative

What is the FAIRTRADE Mark? The FAIRTRADE Mark is an independent consumer label which appears on food products as a guarantee that their producers have had a better deal.

AUFGABE 1

◎ A3.29

| Rezeption: Hörverstehen | 20 Punkte |

Sie sind bei der Byte by Byte GmbH beschäftigt. Sie nehmen für Ihren Kollegen Herrn Bender ein Telefongespräch eines englischsprachigen Geschäftspartners entgegen. Hören Sie aufmerksam zu und fertigen Sie anschließend für Herrn Bender eine entsprechende Gesprächsnotiz auf Deutsch an. Benutzen Sie dazu das untenstehende Formblatt. Hören Sie sich das Gespräch zweimal an.

Byte by Byte GmbH

Gesprächsvermerk

Für: _____

Verfasst von: _____   am: _____

Gesprächspartner: _____

Betrifft: _____

AUFGABE 2

| Rezeption: Leseverstehen | 20 Punkte |

Sie erhalten die Stellenanzeigen auf Seite 127. Ihre Aufgabe besteht darin, sich einen Überblick über die Gemeinsamkeiten und Unterschiede beider Ausschreibungen zu verschaffen. Füllen Sie dazu die Tabelle auf Seite 128 aus.

Sales Advisor – Part-Time 19hrs

Description

Orange Retail staff are a pretty special bunch. For starters, they have boundless energy and an uncanny knack for turning anyone into a valued customer. Then there's their natural drive to sell as many Orange products as humanly possible. And as if that wasn't enough, they are great fun to be with, and we think that's important, too.

Location:	Wrexham
Salary:	Competitive fixed salary with 1% commission, no benefits
Company:	Orange
Job type:	Permanent

Must Haves

To be considered for this role you must be able to demonstrate the following:
- Great listening skills, with the ability to understand and relate to the needs of different customers
- An outgoing and enthusiastic personality
- The desire to reach individual and store targets on a weekly and monthly basis

Nice to Haves

It would be great if you also had some of the following:
- Retail or other frontline customer service experience
- Self motivation and the ability to encourage others

The Department

Our Orange stores are some of the best on the High Street. By building a rapport with customers and providing sound advice, we continually offer what's in the customer's best interests. Whether you are selling phones, explaining tariffs or just engaging in a spot of banter, you are provided with the opportunity to show and explain how customers can get more out of their handsets through our expanding range of lifestyle services. Our stores even have different areas, where customers can do everything from trying out the latest technology, to relaxing within our business section whilst we do all the hard work. It's just about as far from the traditional retail environment as it is possible to be.

Sales Associates – Part-Time

Location:	London
Salary:	Competitive
Company:	Harrods
Job type:	Temporary

Description

Harrods are looking for part-time sales associates to join the various departments from Menswear, Ladieswear, Homewares, Foodhalls and Sports through to Toys, Childrenswear, Furniture and Fashion Accessories.

You will need to have a minimum of 6 months sales experience, and be able to deliver the very best customer service. Working to individual targets, the successful candidate will have fantastic relevant brand knowledge, understanding of the needs of the customer, and a desire to exceed expectations.

Part-time sales associates are required to work between 2 and 4 days per week. You will be expected to work weekends within your monthly rota, with the store open 10 am to 8 pm Monday to Saturday, 12 noon to 6 pm on Sundays. There will also be occasions when you will be required to work later hours during peak sales periods such as Christmas and Sales.

In return for your hard work you will earn a salary of £7.05 per hour, rising after your probationary period (4 months). After your first full calendar month in the business you will also earn 1% commission on all your sales, you will be entitled to a 20% staff discount and 20 days free leave.

Only applicants who can demonstrate the experience we are looking for will be invited to attend an assessment centre here at Harrods.

Quelle: totaljobs.com

Unternehmen	Genaue Stellenbezeichnung	Vergütung	Genaue Arbeitsbeschreibung	Gewünschte Qualifikationen
1. Orange				
2. Harrods				

AUFGABE 3

Produktion   **30 Punkte**

Sie erhalten nachstehendes Organigramm und zwei Grafiken der Firma PharmCom GmbH, einem Unternehmen, das im Bereich der pharmazeutischen Industrie angesiedelt ist. Ihre Aufgabe ist es, für einen englischsprachigen Geschäftsbericht einen zusammenhängenden Text zu verfassen, der die Organisationsstruktur, den Ausbildungshintergrund und die Umsatzentwicklung des Unternehmens in positiver Weise darstellt. Beginnen Sie dabei wie folgt:

PharmCom is a growth-oriented global enterprise aiming to improve quality of life. We are innovative and efficiently organised. At the top of our company ...

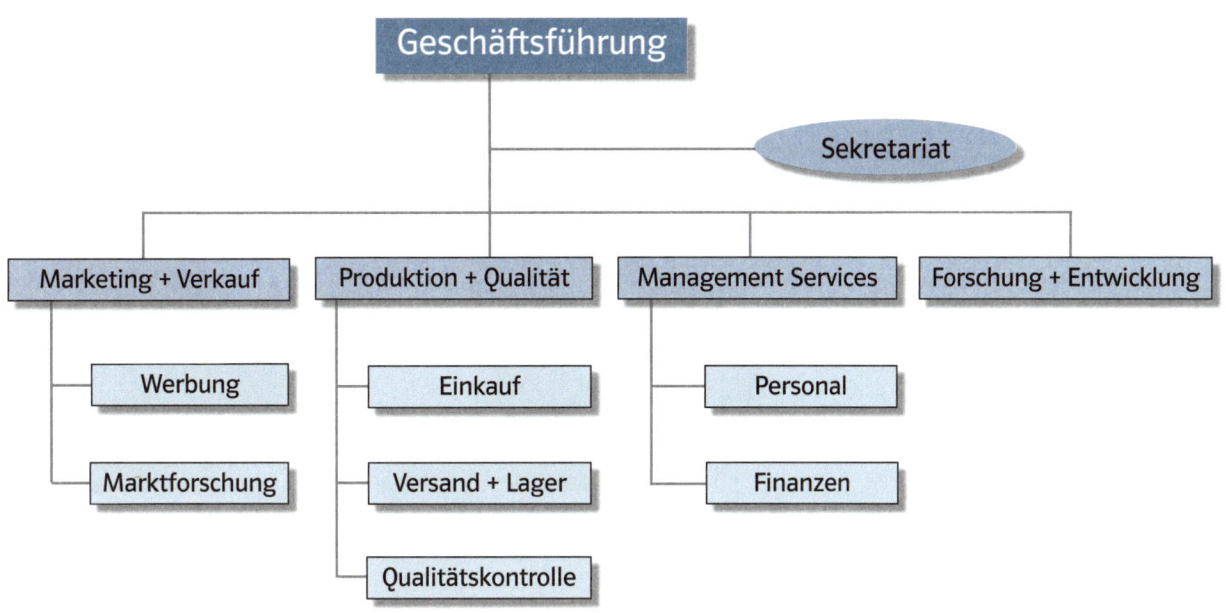

Ausbildungshintergrund der Mitarbeiter

Umsatzentwicklung

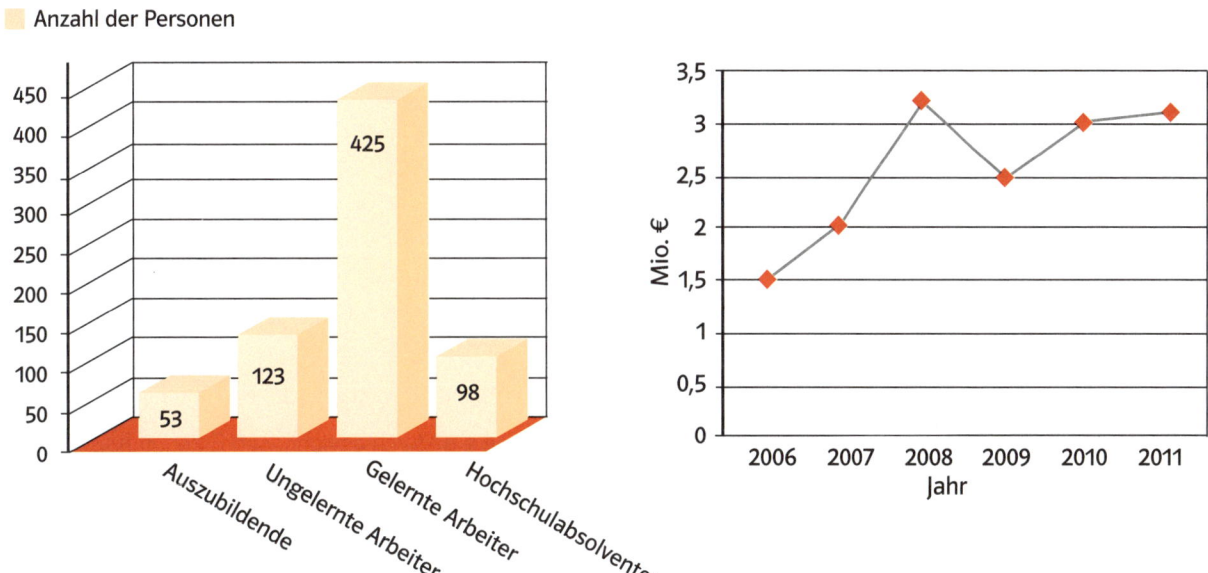

AUFGABE 4

Mediation   **30 Punkte**

Sie arbeiten in einem mittelständischen Unternehmen. Die Homepage des Unternehmens soll künftig auch komplett in Englisch abrufbar sein. Sie erhalten den Auftrag, einen Vorschlag für die Übertragung des Unternehmensleitbildes ins Englische zu erstellen.

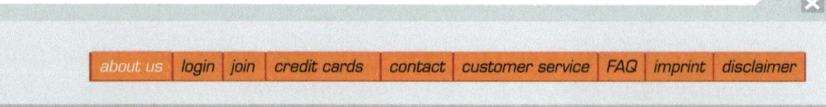

about us | login | join | credit cards | contact | customer service | FAQ | imprint | disclaimer

Unternehmensleitbild

Sowohl die Unternehmensführung als auch die 450 Mitarbeiter haben sich zu einer durch Verantwortung, Kooperation und Respekt geprägten Firmenkultur verpflichtet und folgende Werte zur Maxime ihres täglichen Handels erklärt:

▶ Wir setzen uns herausfordernde Ziele und ziehen alle an einem Strang, um diese zu erreichen.

▶ Wir arbeiten mit Spaß und Leidenschaft und inspirieren dabei unsere Kollegen.

▶ Wir konzentrieren uns auf das Wesentliche.

▶ In unserer täglichen Arbeit verbinden wir Freiheit mit Verantwortung.

▶ Wir würdigen herausragende Arbeit zeitnah durch Lob, Anerkennung und Wertschätzung.

▶ Wir machen verbindliche Zusagen und halten diese ein.

▶ Wir halten uns an unsere Regeln und Standards.

▶ Wir sind bestrebt, Bestehendes kontinuierlich zu verbessern.

▶ Unsere Kunden sind uns wichtig und wir stellen ihre Bedürfnisse in den Fokus unseres Handelns.

▶ Wir unterstützen und motivieren uns gegenseitig und halten zusammen, um gemeinsam erfolgreich zu sein.

▶ Wir sagen das, was zu sagen ist, in angemessener Form, unmittelbar und zu jeder Person.

▶ Wir lernen aus unseren Fehlern und Erfolgen und teilen unsere dadurch gewonnenen Erkenntnisse mit anderen.

Was Sie über die mündliche Prüfung wissen sollten

Neben der schriftlichen Prüfung ist zum Bestehen des KMK-Fremdsprachenzertifikats auch eine mündliche Prüfung vorgeschrieben; beide Prüfungen müssen separat bestanden werden. Die mündliche Prüfung soll als Gruppenprüfung durchgeführt werden, bei der Gespräche persönlichen und berufsfachlichen Inhalts auf Englisch mit mindestens zwei Gesprächspartnern geführt werden.

Bei der mündlichen Prüfung steht die **Interaktion** im Vordergrund. Die Prüflinge sollen einander gut zuhören und aufeinander eingehen, sie sollen sich spontan äußern und versuchen, sich den Gesprächspartnern verständlich zu machen. Ziel ist die gelungene Kommunikation, das heißt dass Sie verstanden werden und auch selbst verstehen. Das bedeutet, dass Sie kleinere Fehler machen können – Hauptsache Sie übermitteln Ihrem Gesprächspartner die Botschaft.

Generell wird von Ihnen auf Stufe I natürlich weniger erwartet als auf Stufe II, auf Stufe II weniger als auf Stufe III, usw. Obwohl die Gesprächsthemen gleich oder ähnlich sein können, werden Sie genau passend zu Ihrer Stufe geprüft.

Was die zeitliche Dauer der mündlichen Prüfung betrifft, so gelten folgende Richtwerte:

KMK Stufe I	15 Minuten pro Gruppenprüfung
KMK Stufe II	20 Minuten pro Gruppenprüfung
KMK Stufe III	25 Minuten pro Gruppenprüfung

Diese Richtwerte beziehen sich auf eine Prüfung mit zwei Prüflingen; bei mehr als zwei Prüflingen kann der Zeitrichtwert entsprechend angepasst werden.

Die mündliche Prüfung besteht in der Regel aus drei Teilen:
1. **Aufwärmphase** zur Vorstellung der eigenen Person oder der eigenen Interessen.
2. **Gelenkter Dialog** im Sinne von Reagieren auf Fragen und Antworten (z. B. Frage-Antwort bei Produktbeschreibung, Telefongespräch als Zickzack-Rollenspiel).
3. **Freier Dialog** (z. B. Beratungsgespräch).

Aufwärmphase

Die Prüflinge werden von den Prüfern gebeten sich z. B. zu folgenden Themen zu äußern:

- hometown
- family
- job
- training company (size, tasks, working hours)
- leisure activities / hobbies / weekend activities
- favourite books / movies / TV programmes

- holidays
- internet / computer
- mobile phone use
- sport
- future plans

Die Aufwärmphase dient Ihnen dazu, Ihre Nervosität abzubauen und ins Sprechen zu kommen. So sollen Sie in den ersten Minuten sicherer werden, um dann zu zeigen, was Sie können.

> **Tipp:**
> Überlegen Sie sich, was Sie über sich selbst erzählen möchten. Schlagen Sie evtl. unbekannte Wörter, wie z. B. Berufsbezeichnung, Produkte Ihres Ausbildungsbetriebes, Sportarten, Hobbies, in einem Wörterbuch oder online nach.

Prüfungsgespräche (gelenkter und freier Dialog)

Prüfungsgespräche haben einen fachlichen Bezug zum Ausbildungsberuf. Es kann um alltägliche berufliche Sachverhalte gehen, es ist aber auch denkbar zwischen einem Sprecher der deutschen Sprache und einem Sprecher der Fremdsprache zu vermitteln. Typische Gesprächssituationen für die Prüfung sind z. B.:

- Kundenkontaktpflege
- Wegbeschreibungen
- Kundenberatungen
- Terminabsprachen
- Gespräche zwischen Kollegen
- Gespräche bei einer Veranstaltung

> **Tipp:**
> Lesen Sie zur Vorbereitung auf die Prüfung nochmals die Übungen zum Smalltalk und zur Vorstellung einer Person durch. Üben Sie mit Freunden, wie man sich selbst vorstellt oder eine andere Person einem Dritten vorstellt. Diese Übung gibt Ihnen Sicherheit bei den Prüfungsgesprächen.

Bewertungskriterien

Die beiden wichtigsten Bewertungskriterien sind die interaktive Kompetenz und die Aufgabenbewältigung. Besonders beachtet wird, ob der Prüfling:

- Hauptinhaltspunkte erkennt
- Vorgaben möglichst präzise umsetzt
- den Gesprächspartner einbezieht
- gezielt auf die Äußerungen des Gesprächspartners eingeht
- Wortwahl und Redewendungen der jeweiligen Situation entsprechend anpasst, insbesondere auf die Kenntnisse des Gesprächspartners eingeht
- auf idiomatisches Englisch und *false friends* achtet
- flüssig, zusammenhängend und gut verständlich spricht
- auf gute Aussprache und grammatikalische Korrektheit achtet

> **Tipp:**
> Vermeiden sollte man einen Gesprächspartner an die Wand zu reden oder ihm ins Wort zu fallen.

MUSTER

Kaufmännische Berufsschule Achtenberg
Hauptstraße 26
77234 Achtenberg

KMK-Fremdsprachenzertifikat

Englisch für Industriekaufmann / frau

**Zertifikat der Ständigen Konferenz der Kultusminister der Länder
in der Bundesrepublik Deutschland zu Fremdsprachen in der beruflichen Bildung**

Frau / Herr   **Nadia Emilia Rehberg**

geboren am   **06. 04. 1992**

hat erfolgreich die Prüfung für dieses Zertifikat
auf Niveaustufe* II (B1)
abgelegt und dabei folgende Ergebnisse erzielt:

I Schriftliche Prüfung	Maximale Punktzahl	Erreichte Punktzahl
1. Texte und gesprochene Mitteilungen verstehen (REZEPTION)	40	31
2. Schriftstücke erstellen (PRODUKTION)	30	26
3. Texte und gesprochene Mitteilungen übertragen (MEDIATION)	30	24
II Mündliche Prüfung		
4. Gespräche führen und / oder dolmetschen (INTERAKTION)	30	27
Gesamtergebnis:	130	108
	(100 %)	83 %
Achtenberg, den 30. 03. 2011		
Schulleiter / -in Dienstsiegel		

* Das Zertifikat entspricht den Anforderungen der Rahmenvereinbarung der Ständigen Konferenz der Kultusminister der Länder in der Bundesrepublik Deutschland vom 20.11.1998 in der Fassung vom 18.06.2008 über die Zertifizierung von Fremdsprachenkenntnissen in der beruflichen Bildung.

Die Prüfung wird in Baden-Württemberg auf drei Niveaustufen (I, II, III) durchgeführt. Diese entsprechen den Kompetenzniveaus A2, B1 und B2 des Gemeinsamen Europäischen Referenzrahmens für Sprachen (GER). Kurze Erläuterung der Kompetenzstufen auf der Rückseite.

Kompetenzbereiche der Niveaustufen I – III (Rückseite des Zertifikats)

In Klammern die Kompetenzstufen des Gemeinsamen Europäischen Referenzrahmens (GER).

Kompetenz-bereich	Niveaustufe I (A2)	Niveaustufe II (B1)	Niveaustufe III (B2)
Rezeption	**Der Prüfling kann** einfach strukturierte berufstypische Texte sowie klar, dialektfrei und langsam gesprochene Mitteilungen nach ggf. wiederholtem Lesen bzw. Hören und unter Einsatz von Hilfsmitteln (z. B. Wörterbüchern und visuellen Darstellungen) auf Einzelinformationen hin auswerten.	**Der Prüfling kann** berufstypische Texte sowie klar und in natürlichem Tempo gesprochenen Mitteilungen nach ggf. wiederholtem Lesen bzw. Hören und unter Einsatz von Hilfsmitteln (wie z. B. Wörterbüchern und visuellen Darstellungen) auf Einzelinformationen hin auswerten.	**Der Prüfling kann** sprachlich anspruchsvollere berufstypische Texte sowie unter Umständen auch dialektgefärbte Mitteilungen ggf. unter Einsatz von Hilfsmitteln (wie z. B. Wörterbüchern und visuellen Darstellungen) auswerten.
Produktion	**Der Prüfling kann** Eintragungen in Formulare des beruflichen Alltags vornehmen und kurze Sätze bilden. Längere Darstellungen gelingen, wenn als Hilfsmittel Wörterbücher und / oder ein Repertoire an Textbausteinen zur Verfügung stehen. Der Prüfling verfügt über die nötigen sprachlichen Mittel, um die im Berufsleben geläufigsten Sachinformationen (wenn auch mit sprachlichen Mängeln) zu übermitteln.	**Der Prüfling kann** berufstypische Standardschriftstücke und mündliche Mitteilungen unter Verwendung von Hilfsmitteln weitgehend korrekt in der Fremdsprache verfassen bzw. formulieren. Berufsbezogene Sachinformationen werden dabei trotz erkennbar eingeschränktem Wortschatz und struktureller Mängel verständlich in der Fremdsprache wiedergegeben.	**Der Prüfling kann** berufstypische Schriftstücke und komplexe mündliche Mitteilungen auch ohne Zuhilfenahme von Textbausteinen insgesamt stil- und formgerecht strukturiert und orthografisch korrekt verfassen bzw. formulieren.
Mediation	**Der Prüfling kann** einen einfachen fremdsprachlich dargestellten Sachverhalt unter Verwendung von Hilfsmitteln auf Deutsch wiedergeben oder einen einfachen auf Deutsch dargestellten Sachverhalt mit eigenen Worten in der Fremdsprache umschreiben.	**Der Prüfling kann** einen fremdsprachlich dargestellten Sachverhalt unter Verwendung von Hilfsmitteln auf Deutsch wiedergeben oder einen in Deutsch dargestellten Sachverhalt mit eigenen Worten in der Fremdsprache umschreiben. Er kann leichte Formen des Dolmetschens und Übersetzens anwenden. Es kommt dabei nicht auf sprachliche und stilistische, sondern nur auf inhaltliche Übereinstimmung an.	**Der Prüfling kann** einen komplexeren fremdsprachlich dargestellten Sachverhalt unter Verwendung von Hilfsmitteln auf Deutsch wiedergeben oder einen komplexeren in Deutsch dargestellten Sachverhalt mit eigenen Worten in der Fremdsprache umschreiben. Er kann leichte Formen des Dolmetschens und Übersetzens anwenden.
Interaktion	**Der Prüfling kann** einfache berufsrelevante Gesprächssituationen unter Mithilfe des Gesprächspartners in der Fremdsprache bewältigen. Er ist dabei sensibilisiert für landestypische Unterschiede in der jeweiligen Berufs- und Arbeitswelt. Er kann auf schriftliche Standardmitteilungen mit einfachen sprachlichen Mitteln reagieren. Aussprache, Wortwahl und Strukturengebrauch können noch stark von der Muttersprache geprägt sein.	**Der Prüfling kann** berufsrelevante Gesprächssituationen unter Einbeziehung des Gesprächspartners in der Fremdsprache bewältigen. Er ist dabei fähig, wesentliche landestypische Unterschiede in der Berufs- und Arbeitswelt zu berücksichtigen. Er kann auf schriftliche Standardmitteilungen reagieren. Aussprache, Wortwahl und Strukturengebrauch können noch von der Muttersprache geprägt sein.	**Der Prüfling kann** berufsrelevante Gesprächssituationen sicher in der Fremdsprache bewältigen und dabei auch die Gesprächsinitiative ergreifen. Er ist dabei fähig, landestypische Unterschiede in der jeweiligen Berufs- und Arbeitswelt angemessen zu berücksichtigen. Er kann auf schriftliche Mitteilungen komplexer Art situationsadäquat reagieren und verfügt über ein angemessenes Ausdrucksvermögen. In Aussprache, Wortwahl und Strukturengebrauch ist die Muttersprache noch erkennbar.

Bildquellennachweis

5 Thinkstock (Stockbyte), München; **5** Thinkstock (iStockphoto), München; **6** Thinkstock (Christopher Robbins), München; **9** Thinkstock (Stockbyte), München; **10** Thinkstock (Ryan McVay), München; **11** Thinkstock (Digital Vision.), München; **14** iStockphoto (Pumba1), Calgary, Alberta; **17** Thinkstock (Jupiterimages), München; **20** Thinkstock (Creatas), München; **20** Fotolia LLC (womue), New York; **21** shutterstock (Monkey Business Images), New York, NY; **23** Thinkstock (Monkey Business Images), München; **24** BigStockPhoto.com (monkeybusinessimages), Davis, CA; **24** Thinkstock (Hemera), München; **27** Thinkstock (Hemera), München; **28** Thinkstock (Jupiterimages), München; **32** shutterstock (Paul Matthew Photography), New York, NY; **33** Thinkstock (Digital Vision), München; **36** Picture-Alliance (Bernd Thissen), Frankfurt; **37** Thinkstock (Digital Vision), München; **41** Thinkstock (Getty Images), München; **45** Thinkstock (iStockphoto), München; **51** MEV Verlag GmbH, Augsburg; **52** Fotolia LLC (Dark Vectorangel), New York; **53** iStockphoto (italianestro), Calgary, Alberta; **53** Thinkstock (iStockphoto), München; **53** Thinkstock (Photos.com), München; **53** Original: Bestand Haus der Geschichte, Bonn; **53** Fotolia LLC (makuba), New York; **53** Fotolia LLC (Fotoali), New York; **53** iStockphoto (RF/David Meharey), Calgary, Alberta; **54** Thinkstock (iStockphoto), München; **56** Fotolia LLC (Rob O'Dea), New York; **57** Thinkstock (Comstock), München; **58** iStockphoto (Chris Schmidt), Calgary, Alberta; **60** shutterstock (Su in Heo), New York, NY; **61** iStockphoto (Cruz Puga), Calgary, Alberta; **62** Thinkstock (Stockbyte), München; **64** Fotolia LLC (Klaus Eppele), New York; **65** Thinkstock (BananaStock), München; **66** Thinkstock (iStockphoto), München; **68** iStockphoto (Judy Ledbetter), Calgary, Alberta; **68** Thinkstock (iStockphoto), München; **68** iStockphoto (tracy tucker), Calgary, Alberta; **68** Thinkstock (Hemera), München; **68** iStockphoto (Damir Spanic), Calgary, Alberta; **68** Fotolia LLC (Michael Flippo), New York; **68** iStockphoto (Svetl), Calgary, Alberta; **68** shutterstock (Katarzyna Krawiec), New York, NY; **69** Picture-Alliance (afp/Morin), Frankfurt; **70** Thinkstock (Photodisc), München; **74** Dreamstime LLC (Iain Mcgillivray), Brentwood, TN; **76** Dreamstime LLC (Julija Sapic), Brentwood, TN; **80** Fotolia LLC (Yuri Arcurs), New York; **80** Avenue Images GmbH (StockDisc), Hamburg; **80** Thinkstock (Photodisc/Jack Hollingsworth), München; **80** Thinkstock (Comstock Images), München; **80** Thinkstock (Stockbyte), München; **81** Fotolia LLC (Yury Shirokov), New York; **84** iStockphoto (RF/Bonita Hein), Calgary, Alberta; **86** Thinkstock (Comstock), München; **88** iStockphoto (Don Bayley), Calgary, Alberta; **93** Robert Bosch GmbH, Stuttgart; **94** MEV Verlag GmbH, Augsburg; **97** shutterstock (K2 images), New York, NY; **98** Thinkstock (iStockphoto/Liza Barry), München; **99** Thinkstock (istockphoto), München; **101** Thinkstock (Hemera), München; **102** Thinkstock (istockphoto), München; **103** iStockphoto (bonnie jacobs), Calgary, Alberta; **105** Robert Bosch GmbH, Stuttgart; **109** Thinkstock (Stockbyte), München; **112** Thinkstock (Stockbyte), München; **113** Fotolia LLC (vgstudio), New York; **114** Ullstein Bild GmbH (Jochen Tack/Imagebroker), Berlin; **117** Messe, Stuttgart; **118** Thinkstock (iStockphoto), München; **120** Thinkstock, München; **121** Alamy Images (Kevin Foy), Abingdon, Oxon; **123** Okapia (Hans Reinhard), Frankfurt; **125** Logo, Stuttgart; **128** Getty Images (John Li), München; **128** Thinkstock (Hemera), München; **130** iStockphoto (Steve Cole), Calgary, Alberta; **131** Thinkstock (istockphoto), München; **133** Klett-Archiv, Stuttgart; **133** Dream Maker Software (RF), Colorado; **COVER** Avenue Images GmbH (Fancy), Hamburg

Textquellennachweis
75 Amazon puts corn flakes on menu, BBC News (http://news.bbc.co.uk); **81** Debit cards are king in the shops, BBC News (http://news.bbc.co.uk); **82** Travel perks trickle down to SMEs, (http://www.timesonline.co.uk); **86** Rebecca Berlin, Choosing the Best Structure for Your Business, (http://www.alllaw.com); **106** SURVEY SHOWS WELCOME IMPROVEMENT BUT RECOVERY STILL FRAGILE, BCC British Chambers of Commerce (www.chamberonline.co.uk); **109** Digital piracy rife, BBC Music News ; **110** Applying for Trade Marks, The Patent Office (www.patent.gov.uk); **118/119** Business Performance Plan, Manchester City Council (www.manchester.gov.uk); **121** Overseas Membership, London Chamber of Commerce and Industry (www.londonchamber.co.uk); **123/124** Smell the coffee, BBC News (www.bbc.co.uk)

Sollte es in einem Einzelfall nicht gelungen sein, den korrekten Rechteinhaber ausfindig zu machen, so werden berechtigte Ansprüche selbstverständlich im Rahmen der üblichen Regelungen abgegolten.

Tracks

Track	Aufgabe	Laufzeit
A3.01	Unit 1, Unit refresher, Aufgabe 2	01:31:16
A3.02	Unit 2, Unit refresher, Aufgabe 3	01:36:09
A3.03	Unit 3, Unit refresher, Aufgabe 3	01:37:74
A3.04	Unit 4, Unit refresher, Aufgabe 3	01:59:72
A3.05	Unit 5, Unit refresher, Aufgabe 3	02:03:21
A3.06	Unit 6, Unit refresher, Aufgabe 2	02:23:15
A3.07	Unit 7, Unit refresher, Aufgabe 2	01:53:01
A3.08	Unit 8, Unit refresher, Aufgabe 2	02:09:09
A3.09	Unit 9, Unit refresher, Aufgabe 3	02:06:58
A3.10	Unit 10, Unit refresher, Aufgabe 2	02:50:23
A3.11	Unit 11, Unit refresher, Aufgabe 2	03:16:54
A3.12	Unit 12, Unit refresher, Aufgabe 2	02:22:72
A3.13	Unit 13, Unit refresher, Aufgabe 2	02:10:68
A3.14	Unit 14, Unit refresher, Aufgabe 2	02:23:13
A3.15	Unit 15, Unit refresher, Aufgabe 2	02:32:20
A3.16	Unit 16, Unit refresher, Aufgabe 3	02:35:43
A3.17	Warm up, Aufgabe 1	01:24:35
A3.18	Übungsaufgabe 1	02:57:57
A3.19	Übungsaufgabe 2	00:49:28
A3.20	Übungsaufgabe 3	00:44:37
A3.21	Übungsaufgabe 4	00:43:68
A3.22	Übungsaufgabe 5	03:41:48
A3.23	Übungsaufgabe 6	03:53:49
A3.24	Übungsaufgabe 7	05:16:59
A3.25	Musterprüfung 1, Aufgabe 1	03:48:59
A3.26	Musterprüfung 1, Aufgabe 1	00:46:65
A3.27	Musterprüfung 2, Aufgabe 1	03:57:39
A3.28	Musterprüfung 3, Aufgabe 1	04:52:71
A3.29	Musterprüfung 4, Aufgabe 1	02:11:52
	Gesamtlaufzeit	70:44:35

Redaktion: Dr. Birgit Reinel, Tübingen
Tontechnik: Klett Studio, Stuttgart und BauerStudios, Ludwigsburg
Presswerk: P+O Compact Disc, Diepholz

Hinweise zur CD-ROM

Auf beiliegender CD-ROM finden Sie Lösungsvorschläge zu allen Aufgaben im Workbook sowie die Audio-Dateien zu:
- Business Milestones: Tracks A1.01–A1.33
- Industry Milestones: Tracks A2.01–A2.04
- Logistics Milestones: Tracks A2.05–A2.14
- Office Milestones: Tracks A2.15–A2.17
- Trade Milestones: Tracks A2.18–A2.23
- Business Milestones Workbook mit Prüfungsvorbereitung KMK-Fremdsprachenzertifikat: Tracks A3.01–A3.29

Inhalt

1 Loesungen.pdf
2 Audio-Tracks

Datei öffnen

1. Legen Sie die CD-ROM in das Laufwerk ein.
2. Öffnen Sie die CD-ROM durch Doppelklick auf das CD Laufwerk (mit Windows Explorer).
3. Die Datei Loesungen.pdf öffnet sich.

Die Audio-Dateien lassen sich auf einem PC abspielen.